The South-West

By A Yankee

Vol. I

by

J. H. Ingraham

Double9 BOOKS

The South-West

By A Yankee

Vol. I

by J. H. Ingraham

ISBN: 978-93-71816-77-9

Published by

DOUBLE 9 BOOKS

2/13-B, Ansari Road
Daryaganj, New Delhi – 110002
info@double9books.com
www.double9books.com
Tel. 011-40042856

ABOUT THE AUTHOR

Joseph Holt Ingraham was born on January 26, 1809, in Portland, Maine, to James Milk Ingraham. Early in life, he spent several years at sea, an experience that likely broadened his worldview and contributed to the vivid narrative settings in his later literary works. After his maritime years, he turned to teaching, working as a language instructor in Mississippi. During the 1840s, he began publishing his writings in various periodicals, including Arthur's Magazine, marking the beginning of a prolific literary career. Ingraham authored numerous novels, many of them historical or religious in nature, characterized by dramatic storytelling and strong moral undertones. His best-known works often focused on biblical settings or themes of spiritual conflict and redemption. On March 7, 1852, he became an Episcopal clergyman, a role that complemented his religious writing and reflected his deepening commitment to theological thought. He continued both his clerical and literary pursuits until his death on December 18, 1860, in Holly Springs, Mississippi. Throughout his life, Ingraham remained dedicated to exploring the intersections of faith, history, and narrative, leaving a lasting mark on American religious and historical fiction.

CONTENTS

TO

THE

HON. JOHN A. QUITMAN,

EX-CHANCELLOR OF MISSISSIPPI,

THESE VOLUMES

ARE

RESPECTFULLY DEDICATED

BY

THE AUTHOR.

I

To be a "Cabin passenger" fifteen or twenty days *out*, in a Yankee merchantman, is to be in a state as nearly resembling that of a half-assoilzied soul in purgatory, as flesh and blood can well be placed in. A meridian sun—a cloudless sky—a sea of glass, like a vast burning reflector, giving back a twin-heaven inverted—a dry, hot air, as though exhaled from a Babylonian furnace, and a deck, with each plank heated to the foot like a plate of hot steel—with the "Horse latitudes," for the scene, might, perhaps, heighten the resemblance.

Zimmerman, in his excellent essay upon Solitude, has described man, in a "state of solitary indolence and inactivity, as sinking by degrees, like stagnant water, into impurity and corruption." Had he intended to describe from experience, the state of man as "Cabin passenger" after the novelty of his new situation upon the heaving bosom of the "dark blue sea," had given place to the tiresome monotony of never-varying, daily repeated scenes, he could not have illustrated it by a more striking figure. This is a state of which you are happily ignorant. Herein, ignorance is the height of bliss, although, should a Yankee propensity for peregrinating stimulate you to become wiser by experience, I will not say that your folly will be more apparent than your wisdom. But if you continue to vegetate in the lovely valley of your nativity, one of "New-England's yeomanry," as you are wont, not a little proudly, to term yourself—burying for that distinctive honour your collegiate laurels beneath the broad-brim of the farmer—exchanging your "gown" for his frock—"Esq." for plain "squire," and the Mantuan's Georgics for those of the Maine Farmer's Almanac—I will cheerfully travel for you; though, as I shall have the benefit of the wear and tear, rubs and bruises—it will be like honey-hunting in our school-boy days, when one fought the bees while the other secured the sweet plunder.

This sea life, to one who is not a sailor, is a sad enough existence—if it may be termed such. The tomb-stone inscription "Hic jacet," becomes prematurely his own, with the consolatory adjunct *et non resurgam*. A condition intermediate between life and death, but more assimilated to the latter than the former, it is passed, almost invariably, in that proverbial inactivity, mental and corporeal, which is the well-known and unavoidable consequence of a long passage. It is a state in which existence is burthensome and almost insupportable, destroying that healthy tone of mind and body, so necessary to the preservation of the economy of the frame of man.—Nothing will so injure a good disposition, as a long voyage. Seeds of impatience and of indolence are there sown, which will be for a long period painfully manifest. The sweetest tempered woman I ever knew, after a passage of sixty days, was converted into a querulous Xantippe; and a gentleman of the most active habits, after a voyage of much longer duration, acquired such indolent ones, that his usefulness as a man of business was for a long time destroyed; and it was only by the strongest application of high, moral energy, emanating from a mind of no common order, that he was at length enabled wholly to be himself again. There is but one antidote for this disease, which should be nosologically classed as *Melancholia Oceana*, and that is employment. But on ship-board, this remedy, like many other good ones on shore, cannot always be found. A meddling, bustling passenger, whose sphere on land has been one of action, and who pants to move in his little circumscribed orbit at sea, is always a "lubberly green horn," or "clumsy marine," in every tar's way—in whose eye the "passenger" is only fit to thin hen-coops, bask in the sun, talk to the helmsman, or, now and then, desperately venture up through the "lubber's hole" to look for *land* a hundred leagues in mid ocean, or, cry "sail ho!" as the snowy mane of a distant wave, or the silvery crest of a miniature cloud upon the horizon, flashes for an instant upon his unpractised vision.

A well-selected library, which is a great luxury at sea, and like most luxuries very rare, does wonders toward lessening this evil; but it is still far from constituting a *panacea*. I know not how it is, unless the patient begins in reality to suspect that he is taking *reading* as a prescription against the foe, and converting his volumes into pill boxes—which by and by gets to be too painfully the truth—but the appetite soon becomes sated, the mind wearied, and the most fascinating and favourite authors "pall upon the sense" with a tiresome familiarity. Reading becomes hateful, for the very reason that it has become necessary. Amusements are exhausted, invented, changed, varied, and again exhausted. Every thing upon which the attention fixes itself, vainly wooing something novel, soon becomes insipid. Chess, back-gammon, letter-writing, journalizing, smoking, eating, drinking, and sleeping, may at first contribute not a little to the discomfiture of old Time, who walks the *sea* shod with leaden sandals. The last three enumerated items, however, generally hold out to the last undisabled. But three Wellingtons could not have won Waterloo unsupported; nor, able and doughty as are these bold three—much as they prolong the combat—manfully as they fight, can they hold good their ground for ever; the obstinate, scythe-armed warrior, with his twenty-four body guards following him like his shadow, will still maintain the broadest portion of his diurnal territory, over which, manœuvre as they may, these discomfited worthies cannot extend their front.

Few situations are less enviable, than that of the worn voyager, as day after day "drags its slow length along," presenting to his restless, listless eyes, as he stretches them wearily over the leaden waste around him—the same unbroken horizon, forming the periphery of a circle, of which his vessel seems to be the immovable and everlasting centre—the same blue, unmeaning skies above—the same blue sea beneath and around—the same gigantic tracery of ropes and spars, whose fortuitous combinations of strange geometrical figures he has demonstrated, till they are as familiar as the diagrams on a turtle's back to an alderman; and the same dull white sails, with whose patches he has become as familiar as with the excrescences and other innocent defects upon the visages of his fellow-sufferers.

On leaving port, I commenced a journal, or rather, as I am in a nautical atmosphere, a "log," the choicest chips of which shall be hewn off, basketed in fools-cap, and duly transmitted to you. Like other chips they may be useful to kindle the fire withal. "What may not warm the feelings may—the toes," is a truism of which you need not be reminded: and if you test it practically, it will not be the first time good has been elicited from evil. But the sameness of a sea-life will by no means afford me many combustible incidents. Somebody has said "the will is equal to the deed, if the deed cannot be." Now I have the will to pile a hecatomb, but if I can pile only a couple of straws, it will be, of course, the same thing in the abstract. Mine, perchance, may be the fate of that poor journalist who, in a voyage across the Atlantic, could obtain but one wretched item wherewith to fill his journal—which he should have published, by the way. What a rare sort of a book it would have been! So soon read too! In this age when type-blotted books are generative, it would immortalize the author. Tenderly handed down from one generation to another, it would survive the "fall of empires, and the crash of worlds." "At three and a quarter P. M., ship going two and a half knots per hour, the cook lost his bucket over-board—jolly boat lowered, and Jack and Peter rowed after it."

"Half-past three, P. M.—Cook has got his bucket again—and a broken head into the bargain."

To one who has never "played with Ocean's mane," nor, borne by his white-winged coursers, scoured his pathless fields, there may be, even in the common-place descriptions of sea-scenes, something, which wears the charm of novelty. If my hasty sketches can contribute to your entertainment "o' winter nights," or, to the gratification of your curiosity, they will possess an influence which I do not promise or predict for them.

Unfavourable winds had detained our ship several days, and all who had taken passage were on the "tiptoe of expectation" for the signal for sailing. Trunks, boxes, chests, cases, carpet-bags, and all the paraphernalia of travelling equipage, had long been packed, locked, and shipped—and our eyes had hourly watched the fickle gyrations of a horizontal gilt figure, which surmounted the spire of a neighbouring church, till they ached again. Had the image been Eolus himself, it could not have commanded more devoted worshippers.

A week elapsed—and patience, which hitherto had been admirably sustained, began to flag; murmurings proceeded from the lips of more than one of the impatient passengers, as by twos and threes, they would meet by a kind of sympathetic affinity at the corners of the streets, where an unobstructed view could be obtained of some church-vane, all of which, throughout our city of churches, had taken a most unaccommodating fancy to kick their golden-shod heels at the Northern Bear.

At precisely twenty minutes before three of the clock, on the afternoon of the first of November instant, the phlegmatic personage in the gilt robe, very obligingly, after he had worn our patience to shreds by his obstinacy, let his head and heels exchange places. At the same moment, ere he had ceased vibrating and settled himself steadily in his new position, the welcome signal was made, and in less than half an hour afterward, we were all, with bag and baggage, on board the ship, which rode at her anchor two hundred fathoms from the shore.

The top-sails, already loosed, were bellying and wildly collapsing with a loud noise, in the wind; but bounding to their posts at the command of their superior officer, the active seamen soon extended them upon the spars—immense fields of swelling canvass; and our vessel gracefully moved from her moorings, and glided through the water with the lightness of a swan.

As we moved rapidly down the noble harbour, which, half a century since, bore upon its bosom the hostile fleet of the proud island of the north, the swelling ocean was sending in its evening tribute to the continent, in vast scrolls, which rolled silently, but irresistibly onward, and majestically unfolded upon the beach—or, with a hoarse roar, resounded along the cliffs, and surged among the rocky throats of the promontory, impressing the mind with emotions of sublimity and awe.

II

The motion was just sufficiently lively to inspirit one—making the blood frolic through the veins, and the heart beat more proudly. The old tars, as they cruised about the decks, walked as steadily as on land. This proves nothing, you may say, if you have witnessed Jack's pendulating, uncertain—"right and left oblique" advance on a shore cruise.

Our tyros of the sea, in their venturesome projections of their persons from one given point in their eye to another, in the hope of accomplishing a straight line, after vacillating most appallingly, would finally succeed "haud passibus æquis" in reaching the position aimed for, fortunate if a lee-lurch did not accommodate them with a dry bed in the "lee scuppers."

Of all laughter-exciting locomotives which most create sensations of the ludicrously serious, commend me to an old land-crab teaching its young one to "go *ahead*"—a drunkard, reeling homeward through a broad street on a Saturday night—and a "gentleman passenger" three days at sea in his strange evolutions over the deck.

Stretched before me upon the weather hen-coop, enveloped in his cloak, lay one of our "goodlie companie." If his sensations were such as I imagined them to be, he must have felt that the simplest chicken under him wore the stoutest heart.

On the lee hen-coop reposed another passenger in sympathy with his fellow, to whose feelings I felt a disposition to do equal justice. Abaft the wheel, coiled up in the rigging, an agreeable substitute for a bed of down, lay half obscured within the shadow of the lofty stern, another overdone toper—a victim of Neptune, not of the "jolly god"—but whose sensations have been experienced by many of the latter's pupils, who have never tasted other salt water than their own tears.

It has been said or sung by some one, that the "ear is the road to the heart." That it was so to the stomach, I already began to feel, could not be disputed; and as certain "guttural sounds" began to multiply from various quarters, with startling emphasis, lest I should be induced to sympathize with the fallen novitiates around me, by some *overt* act, I hastily glided by the helmsman, who stood alone like the sole survivor of a battle-field—his weather-beaten visage illuminated at the moment with a strange glare from the "binnacle-lamp" which, concealed within a case like a single-windowed pigeon house, and open in front of him, burned nightly at his feet. The next moment I was in the cabin, now lighted up by a single lamp suspended from the centre of the ceiling, casting rather shade than light upon a small table—studiously arranged for supper by the steward—that non-descript *locum tenens* for valet—waiter—chambermaid—shoe-black—cook's-mate, and swearing-post for irascible captains to vent stray oaths upon, when the wind is ahead—with a flying commission for here, there, and nowhere! when most wanted.

But the supper! ay, the supper. Those for whom the inviting display was made, were, I am sorry to say it, most unhesitatingly "floored" and quite *hors du combat*. What a deal of melancholy truth there is in that aphorism, which teaches us that the "brave must yield to the braver!"

As I stood beside the helmsman, I could feel the gallant vessel springing away from under me, quivering through every oaken nerve, like a high-mettled racer with his goal but a bound before him. As she encountered some more formidable wave, there would be a tremendous outlay of animal-like energy, a momentary struggle, a half recoil, a plunging, trembling—*onward* rush—then a triumphant riding over the conquered foe, scattering the gems from its shivered crest in glittering showers over her bows. Then gliding with velocity over the glassy concave beyond, swaying to its up-lifting impulse with a graceful inclination of her lofty masts, and almost sweeping the sea with her yards, she would majestically recover herself in time to gather power for a fresh victory.

Within an hour after clearing the last head-land, whose lights, level with the plain of the sea, gleamed afar off, twinkling and lessened like stars, with which they were almost undistinguishably mingled on the horizon—we had exchanged the abrupt, irregular "seas" of the bay, for the regular, majestically rolling billows of the ocean.

I had been for some time pacing the deck, with the "officer of the watch" to recover my sea-legs, when the helmsman suddenly shouted in a wild startling cry, heard, mingling with the wind high above the booming of the sea, the passing hour of the night watch.—"Four bells."—"Four bells," repeated the only one awake on the forecastle, and the next moment the ship's bell rung out loud and clear—wildly swelling upon the gale, then mournfully dying away in the distance as the toll ceased, like the far-off strains of unearthly music—

"—— Died the solemn knell
As a trumpet music dies,

By the night wind borne away
Through the wild and stormy skies."

There is something so awful in the loud voice of a man mingling with the deep tones of a bell, heard at night upon the sea, that familiar as my ear was with the sounds—the blood chilled at my heart as this "lonely watchman's cry" broke suddenly upon the night.

When he again told the hour I was safely stowed away in a comfortable berth, not so large as that of Goliah of Gath by some cubits, yet admirably adapted to the sea, which serves most discourteously the children of Somnus, unless they fit their berths like a modern M. D. his sulkey, lulled to sleep by the rattling of cordage, the measured tread of the watch directly over me, the moanings, *et cætera*, of sleepless neighbours, the roaring of the sea, the howling of the wind, and the gurgling and surging of the water, as the ship rushed through it, shaking the waves from her sides, as the lion scatters the dew from his mane, and the musical rippling of the eddies—like a glassichord, rapidly run over by light fingers—curling and singing under the keel.

III

"Let's whip these stragglers o'er the seas again," was the gentle oratory of the aspiring Richard, in allusion to the invading Bretagnes.—

"Lash hence these overweening rags of France."

The interpreter of the heart's natural language—Shakspeare, above all men, was endowed with human inspiration. His words come ripe to our lips like the fruit of our own thoughts. We speak them naturally and unconsciously. They drop from us like the unpremeditated language of children—spring forth unbidden—the richest melody of the mind. Strong passion, whether of grief or joy while seeking in the wild excitement of the moment her own words for utterance, unconsciously enunciates *his*, with a natural and irresistible energy. There is scarcely a human thought, great or simple, which Shakspeare has not spoken for his fellow-men, as never man, uninspired, spake; which he has not embodied and clothed with a drapery of language, unsurpassable. So—

"Let's whip *this* straggler o'er the seas again,"

I have very good reason to fear, will flow all unconsciously from your lips, as most applicable to my barren letter; in penning which I shall be driven to extremity for any thing of an interesting character. If it must be so, I am, of all epistlers, the most innocent.

Ship, air, and ocean equally refuse to furnish me with a solitary incident. My wretched "log" now and then records an event: such as for instance, how one of "the Doctor's" plumpest and most deliriously *embonpoint* pullets, very rashly and unadvisedly perpetrated a summerset over-board, after she had been decapitated by that sable gentleman, in certainly the most approved and scientific style. None but a very silly chicken could have been dissatisfied with the unexceptionable manner in which the operation was performed. But, both feathered and plucked bipeds, it seems, it is equally hard to please.

For the last fourteen days we have been foot-balls for the winds and waves. Their game may last as many more; therefore, as we have as little free agency in our movements as foot-balls themselves, we have made up our minds to yield our fretted bodies as philosophically as may be, to their farther pastime. The sick have recovered, and bask the hours away on deck in the beams of the warm south sun, like so many luxurious crocodiles.

To their good appetites let our table bear witness. Should it be blessed with a conscience, it is doubly blessed by having it cleared thrice daily by the most rapacious father-confessors that ever shrived penitent; of which "gentlemen of the *cloth*" it boasts no less than eight.

The first day we passed through a widely dispersed fleet of those short, stump-masted *non-descripts*, with swallow-tailed sterns, snubbed bows, and black hulls, sometimes denominated fishing smacks, but oftener and more euphoniously, "Chebacco boats," which, from May to October, are scattered over our northern seas.

While we dashed by them, one after another, in our lofty vessel, as, close-hauled on the wind, or "wing and wing," they flew over the foaming sea, I could not help smiling at the ludicrous scenes which some of their decks exhibited.

One of them ran so close to us, that we could have tossed a potato into the "skipper's" dinner-pot, which was boiling on a rude hearth of bricks placed upon the open deck, under the *surveillance* of, I think, the veriest mop-headed, snub-nosed bit of an urchin that I ever saw.

"Keep away a little, or you'll run that fellow down," suddenly shouted the captain to the helmsman; and the next moment the little fishing vessel shot swiftly under our stern, just barely clearing the spanker boom, whirling and bouncing about in the wild swirl of the ship's wake like a "Massallah boat" in the surf of Madras.

There were on board of her four persons, including the steersman—a tall, gaunt old man, whose uncovered gray locks streamed in the wind as he stooped to his little rudder to luff up across our wake. The lower extremities of a loose pair of tar-coated duck trowsers, which he wore, were incased, including the best part of his legs, in a pair of fisherman's boots, made of leather which would flatten a rifle ball. His red flannel shirt left his hairy breast exposed to the icy winds, and a huge pea-jacket, thrown, Spanish fashion, over his shoulders, was fastened at the throat by a single button. His tarpaulin—a little narrow-brimmed hat of the pot-lid tribe, secured by a ropeyarn—had probably been thrown off in the moment of danger, and now hung swinging by a lanyard from the lower button-hole of his jacket.

As his little vessel struggled like a drowning man in the yawning concave made by the ship, he stood with one hand firmly grasping his low, crooked rudder, and with the other held the main sheet, which alone he tended. A short pipe protruded from his mouth, at which he puffed away incessantly; one eye was tightly closed, and the other was so contracted within a network of wrinkles, that I could just discern the twinkle of a gray pupil, as he cocked it up at our quarter-deck, and took in with it the noble size, bearing, and apparel of our fine ship.

A duplicate of the old helmsman, though less battered by storms and time, wearing upon his chalky locks a red, woollen, conical cap, was "easing off" the foresheet as the little boat passed; and a third was stretching his neck up the companion ladder, to stare at the "big ship," while the little carroty-headed imp, who was just the old skipper *razeed*, was performing the culinary operations of his little kitchen under cover of the heavens.

Our long pale faces tickled the young fellow's fancy extremely.

"Dad," squalled the youthful reprobate, in the softest, hinge-squeaking soprano—"Dad, I guess as how them ar' chaps up thar, ha'nt lived on salt grub long."—The rascal—we could have minced him with his own fish and potatoes.

"Hold your yaup, you youngster you," roared the old man in reply.—The rest of the beautiful alliteration was lost in the distance, as his smack bounded from us, carrying the young *sans-culotte* out of reach of the consequences of his temerity. To mention *salt grub* to men of our stomachs' capacity, at that moment! He merited impaling upon one of his own cod-hooks. In ten minutes after, we could just discern the glimmer of the little vessel's white sails on the verge of the distant horizon, in whose hazy hue the whole fleet soon disappeared.

These vessels were on a tardy return from their Newfoundland harvests, which, amid fogs and squalls, are gathered with great toil and privation between the months of May and October. The fishermen constitute a distinct and peculiar class—not of society, but of men. To you I need not describe them. They are to be seen at any time, and in great numbers, about the wharves of New-England sea-ports in the winter season—weather-browned, long-haired, coarsely garbed men, with honesty and good nature stamped upon their furrowed and strongly marked features. They are neither "seamen" nor "countrymen," in the usual signification of these words, but a compound of both; combining the careless, free-and-easy air of the one, with the awkwardness and simplicity of the other. Free from the grosser vices which characterize the foreign-voyaged *sailor*, they seldom possess, however, that religious tone of feeling which distinguishes the ruder *countryman*.

Marblehead and Cape Cod are the parent nurseries of these hardy men. Portland has, however, begun to foster them, thereby adding a new and vigorous sinew to her commercial strength. In conjunction with the whale fisheries, to which the cod are a sort of introductory school, these fisheries are the principal nurseries of American seamen. I have met with many American ships' crews, one-half or two-thirds of which were composed of men who had served their apprenticeship in the "fisheries." The youth and men whom they send forth are the bone and muscle of our navy. They have an instinctive love for salt water. Every one who is a parent, takes his sons, one after another, as they doff their petticoats, if the freedom of their limbs was ever restrained by such unnecessary appendages, and places them on the deck of his fishing smack; teaches them to call the ropes by their names, bait, fling, and patiently watch the deceptive hook, and dart the harpoon, or plunge the grains—just as the Indian is accustomed to lead his warrior-boys forth to the hunting grounds, and teach them to track the light-footed game, or heavier-heeled foe—wing, with unerring aim, the fatal arrow, or launch the deadly spear.

The three succeeding days we were delayed by calms, or contending with gales and head winds. On the morning of the seventh day "out," there was a general exclamation of surprise from the passengers as they came on deck.

"How warm!" "What a suffocating air!" "We must have sailed well last night to be so far south!" They might well have been surprised if this change in the temperature had been gained by regular "southing." But, alas, we had barely lessened our latitude twenty miles during the night. We had entered the Gulf Stream! that extraordinary natural phenomenon of the Atlantic Ocean. This immense circle of tepid water which revolves in the Atlantic, enclosing within its periphery, the West India and Western Islands, is supposed by Humboldt to be occasioned "by the current of rotation (trade winds) which strikes against the coasts of Veraguas and Honduras, and ascending toward the Gulf of Mexico, between Cape Caloche and Cape St. Antoine, issues between the Bahamas and Florida." From this point of projection, where it is but a few miles wide, it spreads away to the northeast in the shape of an elongated slightly curved fan, passing at the distance of about eighty miles from the coast of the southern states, with a velocity, opposite Havana, of about four miles an hour, which decreases in proportion to its distance from this point. Opposite Nantucket, where it takes a broad, sweeping curve toward Newfoundland, it moves generally only about two miles an hour. Bending from Newfoundland through the Western Islands, it loses much of its velocity at this distance from its radiating point, and in the eastern Atlantic its motion is scarcely perceptible, except by a slight ripple upon the surface.

This body of water is easily distinguishable from that of the surrounding blue ocean by its leaden hue—the vast quantity of pale-yellow gulf-weed, immense fields of which it wafts from clime to clime upon its ever-rolling bosom, and by the absence of that phosphorescence, which is peculiar to the waters of the ocean. The water of this singular stream is many degrees warmer than the sea through which it flows. Near Cuba the heat has been ascertained to be as great as 81°, and in its course northward from Cuba, it loses 2° of temperature for every 3° of latitude. Its warmth is easily accounted for as the production of very simple causes. It receives its original impulse in the warm tropical seas, which, pressed toward the South American shore by the wind, meet with resistance and are deflected along the coast northward, as stated above by Humboldt, and injected into the Northern Atlantic Ocean—the vast column of water having parted with very little of its original caloric in its rapid progress.

We crossed the north-western verge of "The Gulf" near the latitude of Baltimore, where its breadth is about eighty miles. The atmosphere was sensibly warmer here than that of the ocean proper, and the water which we drew up in the ship's bucket raised the mercury a little more than 8°. Not knowing how the mercury stood before entering the Gulf, I could not determine accurately the change in the atmosphere; but it must have been very nearly as great as that in the denser fluid. Veins of cool air circled through its atmosphere every few minutes, as welcome and refreshing to our bared foreheads as the sprinkling of the coolest water.

When vessels in their winter voyages along our frigid coasts become coated with ice, so as to resemble almost precisely, though of a gigantic size, those miniature glass ships so often seen preserved in transparent cases, they seek the genial warmth of this region to "thaw out," as this dissolving process is termed by the sailors. We were nearly three days in crossing the Gulf, at a very acute angle with its current, which period of time we passed very pleasantly, for voyagers; as we had no cold weather to complain of, and a variety of objects to entertain us. Sea, or Gulf-weed, constantly passed us in acres, resembling immense meadows of harvest wheat, waving and undulating with the breeze, tempting us to walk upon it. But for the ceaseless roll and pitching of our ship, reminding us of our where-about, we might, without much trouble, have been cheated into the conviction that it was real *terra firma*.

Flocks of flying fish suddenly breaking from a smooth, swelling billow, to escape the jaws of some voracious pursuer, whose dorsal fin would be seen protruding for an instant afterward from the surface, flitted swiftly, with a skimming motion, over the sea, glittering in the sun like a flight of silver-winged birds; and then as suddenly, with dried wings, dropped into the sea again. One morning we found the decks sprinkled with these finned aerial adventurers, which had flown on board during the night.

Spars, covered with barnacles—an empty barrel marked on the head N. E. Rum, which we slightly altered our course *to speak*—a hotly contested *affaire d'honneur*, between two bantam-cocks in the weather-coop—a few lessons in splicing and braiding sennet, taken from a good-natured old sailor—a few more in the art of manufacturing "Turks' Heads," not, however, *à la Grec*—and other matters and things equally important, also afforded subjects of speculation and chit-chat, and means of passing away the time with a tolerable degree of comfort, and, during the intervals of eating and sleeping, to keep us from the blues.

A gallant ship—a limitless sea rolled out like a vast sheet of mottled silver—"goodlie companie"—a warm, reviving sun—a flowing sheet, and a courteous breeze, so gently breathing upon our sails, that surly Boreas, in a gentler than his wonted mood, must have sent a bevy of Zephyrs to waft us along—are combinations which both nautical amateurs and ignoramuses know duly how to appreciate.

From the frequency of "squalls" and "blows" off Hatteras, it were easy to imagine a telegraphic communication existing between that head-land and Bermuda, carried on by flashes of lightning and tornadoes; or a game at bowls between Neptune and Boreas, stationed one on either spot, and hurling thunderbolts over the sea. This region, and that included between 25° and 23° north latitude termed by sailors the "horse latitudes," are two of the most unpleasant localities a voyager has to encounter on his passage from a New-England sea-port to New-Orleans or Havana. In one he is wearied by frequent calms, in the other, exposed to sea sickness, and terrified by almost continual storms.

On the eighth day out, we passed Bermuda—that island-sentinel and spy of Britain upon our shores. The position of this post with regard to America, forcibly reminds me—I speak it with all due reverence for the "Lion" of England—of a lap-dog sitting at a secure distance and keeping guard over an eagle *volant*. How like proud England thus to come and set herself down before America, and like a still beautiful mother, watch with a jealous eye the unfolding loveliness of her rival daughter—build up a battery d'espionage against her shores, and seek to hold the very key of her seas.

The Bermudas or "Summer islands" so called from Sir George Summer, who was wrecked here two centuries since—are a cluster of small coral reefs lying nearly in the form of a crescent, and walled round and defended from the sea by craggy rocks, which rear their fronts on every side like battlements:—They are situated about two hundred and twenty leagues from the coast of South Carolina, and nearly in the latitude of the city of Charleston.

The houses are constructed of porous limestone, not unlike lava in appearance. This material was probably ejected by some unseen and unhistoried volcanic eruption, by which the islands themselves were in all probability heaved up from the depths of the ocean. White-washed to resist the rain, their houses contrast beautifully with the green-mantled cedars and emerald carpets of the islands. The native Bermudians follow the sea for a livelihood. They make good sailors while at sea; but are dissipated and indolent when they return to their native islands, indulging in drinking, gaming, and every species of extravagance.

The females are rather pretty than otherwise; with good features and uncommonly fine eyes. Like all their sex, they are addicted to dress, in which they display more finery than taste. Dancing is the pastime of which they are most passionately fond. In affection and obedience to their "lords," and in tenderness to their children, it is said that they are patterns to all fair ones who may have taken those, seldom *audibly-spoken*, vows, "to love, honour, and obey"—oft times unuttered, I verily believe, from pure intention.

St. George, the principal town in the islands, has become a fashionable military residence. The society, which is English and extremely agreeable, is varied by the constant arrival and departure of ships of war, whose officers, with those of the army, a sprinkling of distinguished civilians, and clusters of fair beings who have winged it over the sea, compose the most spirited and pleasant society in the world. Enjoying a remarkably pure air, and climate similar to that of South Carolina, with handsomely revenued clergymen of the Church of England, and rich in various tropical luxuries, it is a desirable foreign residence and a convenient and pleasant haven for British vessels sailing in these seas.

This morning we were all in a state of feverish excitement, impatient to place our eyes once more upon land. Visions of green fields and swelling hills, pleasantly waving trees and cool fountains—groves, meadows, and rural cottages, had floated through our waking thoughts and mingled with our dreams.

"Is the land in sight, Captain?" was the only question heard from the lips of one and another of the expectant passengers as they rubbed their sleepy eyes, poked their heads from their half-opened state-room doors, or peeped from their curtained berths. Ascending to the deck, we beheld the sun just rising from the sea in the splendor of his oriental pomp, flinging his beams far along the sky and over the waters, enriching the ocean with his radiance till it resembled a sea of molten gold, gilding the dew-hung spars, and spreading a delicate blush of crimson over the white sails. It was a morning of unrivalled beauty. But thanks to nautical housewifery, its richness could not be enjoyed from the decks.

At sea, the moment the sun rises, and when one feels in the humor of quitting his hot state-room and going on deck, the officer of the watch sings out in a voice that goes directly to the heart—"Forard there—wash decks!" Then commences an elemental war rivalling Noah's deluge. *That* was caused by the pouring down of rain in drops—*thié* by the out-pouring of full buckets. From the moment this flood commences one may draw back into his narrow shell, like an affrighted snail, and take a morning's nap:—the deck, for an hour to come, is no place for animals that are not web-footed.

Fore and aft the unhappy passenger finds no way of escaping the infliction of this purifying ceremony. Should he be driven aloft, there "to banquet on the morning," he were better reposing on a gridiron or sitting astride a handsaw. If below, there the steward has possession, sweeping, laying the breakfast table and making-up berths, and the air, a hundred times breathed over, rushes from the opening state-rooms threatening to suffocate him—he were better engulfed in the bosom of a stew-pan.

To stand, cold, wet, and uncomfortable upon the damp decks till the sun has dried both them and him is the only alternative. If after all the "holy stone" should come in play, he may then quietly jump over-board.

The evenings, however, amply compensate for the loss of the fine mornings. The air, free from the dust, floating particles and exhalations of the land, is perfectly transparent, and the sky of a richer blue. The stars seem nearer to you there; and the round moon pours her unclouded flood of light, down upon the sea, with an opulence and mellowness, of which those who have only seen moonlight, sleeping upon green hills, cities and forests, know nothing. On such nights, there cannot be a nobler, or prouder spectacle, as one stands upon the bows, than the lofty, shining pyramid of snow-white canvass which, rising majestically from the deck, lessens away, sail after sail, far into the sky—each sheet distended like a drum-head, yet finely rounded, and its towering summit, as the ship rises and falls upon the billows, waving like a tall poplar, swaying in the wind. In these hours of moonlit enchantment, while reclining at full length upon the deck, and gazing at the diminished point of the flag-staff, tracing devious labyrinths among the stars, the blood has danced quicker through my veins as I could feel the ship springing away beneath me like a fleet courser, and leaping from wave to wave over the sea. At such moments the mind cannot divest itself of the idea that the bounding ship is instinct with life—an animated creature, careering forward by its own volition. To this are united the musical sighing of the winds through the sails and rigging—the dashing of the sea and the sound of the rushing vessel through the water, which sparkles with phosphorescent light, as though sprinkled with silver dust.

A dark night also affords a scene to gratify curiosity and charm the eye. A few nights since, an exclamation of surprise from one of the passengers called me from my writing to the deck. As, on emerging from the cabin, I mechanically cast my eyes over the sea, I observed that at first it had the appearance of reflecting the stars from its bosom in the most dazzling splendour, but on looking upward to gaze upon the original founts of this apparently reflected light, my eyes met only a gloomy vault of clouds unillumined by a solitary star. The "scud" flew wildly over its face and the heavens were growing black with a gathering tempest. Yet beneath, the sea glittered like a "lake of fire." The crests of the vast billows as they burst high in the air, descended in showers of scintillations. The ship scattered broken light from her bows, as though a pavement of mirrors had been shivered in her pathway. Her track was marked by a long luminous train, not unlike the tail of a comet, while gleams of light like lighted lamps floating upon the water, whirled and flashed here and there in the wild eddies of her wake. The spray which was flung over the bows glittered like a sprinkling of diamonds as it fell upon the decks, where, as it flowed around the feet, it sparkled for some seconds with innumerable shining specks. And so intense was the light shining from the sea that I was enabled to read with ease the fine print of a newspaper. A bucket plunged into the sea, which whitened like shivered ice, on its striking it, was drawn up full of glittering sea-water that sparkled for more than a minute, after being poured over the deck, and then gradually losing its lustre, finally disappeared in total darkness.

Many hypotheses have been suggested by scientific men to account for this natural phenomenon. "Some have regarded it," says Dr. Coates, "as the effect of electricity, produced by the friction of the waves; others as the product of a species of fermentation in the water, occurring accidentally in certain places. Many have attributed it to the well-known phosphorescence of putrid fish, or to the decomposition of their slime and exuviæ, and a few only to the real cause, the voluntary illumination of many distinct species of marine animals.

"The purpose for which this phosphorescence is designed is lost in conjecture; but when we recollect that fish are attracted to the net by the lights of the fisherman, and that many of the marine shellfish are said to leave their native element to crawl around a fire built upon the beach, are we not warranted in supposing that the animals of which we have been speaking, are provided with these luminous properties, in order to entice their prey within their grasp?"

IV

"Land ho!" shouted a voice both loud and long, apparently from the clouds, just as we had comfortably laid ourselves out yesterday afternoon for our customary *siesta*.

"Where away?" shouted the captain, springing to the deck, but not so fast as to prevent our tumbling over him, in the head-and-heels projection of our bodies up the companion-way, in our eagerness to catch a glimpse, once more, of the grassy earth; of something at least stationary.

"Three points off the weather bow," replied the man aloft.

"Where is it?"—"which way?" "I see it"—"Is that it captain—the little hump?" were the eager exclamations and inquiries of the enraptured passengers, who, half beside themselves, were peering, straining, and querying, to little purpose.

It was Abaco—the land first made by vessels bound to New Orleans or Cuba, from the north. With the naked eye, we could scarcely distinguish it from the small blue clouds, which, resting, apparently, on the sea, floated near the verge of the southern horizon. But with the spy glass, we could discern it more distinctly, and less obscured by that vail of blue haze, which always envelopes distant objects when seen from a great distance at sea, or on land.

As we approached, its azure vail gradually faded away, and it appeared to our eyes in its autumnal gray coat, with all its irregularities of surface and outline clearly visible.

Slightly altering our course, in order to weather its southern extremity, we ran down nearly parallel with the shores of the island that rose apparently from the sea, as we neared it, stretching out upon the water like a huge alligator, which it resembled in shape. Sail after sail hove in sight as we coasted pleasantly along with a fine breeze, till, an hour before the sun went down, a large wide-spreading fleet could be discerned from the deck, lying becalmed, near the extreme southern point of Abaco, which, stretching out far into the sea, like a wall perforated with an arched gateway near the centre, is better known by the familiar appellation of "The Hole in the Wall."

"There is a habitation of some sort," exclaimed one of the passengers, whose glass had long been hovering over the island.

"Where—where?" was the general cry, and closer inspection from a dozen eyes, detected a miserable hut, half hidden among the bushes, and so wild and wretched in appearance, that we unanimously refused it the honor of

"——A local habitation and a name!"

It was nevertheless the first dwelling of man we had seen for many a day; and notwithstanding our vote of non-acceptance, it was not devoid of interest in our eyes. It was evidently the abode of some one of those demi sea-monsters, called "Wreckers," who, more destructive than the waves, prey upon the ship-wrecked mariner. The Bahamas swarm with these wreckers who, in small lugger-sloops, continually prowl about among the islands,

"When the demons of the tempest rave,"

like birds of ill omen, ready to seize upon the storm-tossed vessel, should it be driven among the rocks or shoals with which this region abounds. At midnight, when the lightning for a moment illumines the sky and ocean, the white sail of the wrecker's little bark, tossing amid the storm upon the foaming billows, will flash upon the eyes of the toiling seamen as they labour to preserve their vessel, striking their souls with dread and awakening their easily excited feelings of superstition. Like evil spirits awaiting at the bed-side the release of an unannealed soul, they hover around the struggling ship through the night, and, flitting away at the break of morning, may be discovered in the subsiding of the tempest, just disappearing under the horizon with a sailor's hearty blessing sent after them.

That light-houses have not been erected on the dangerous head-lands and reefs which line the Bahama channel, is a strange oversight or neglect on the part of the governments of the United States and England, which of all maritime nations are most immediately concerned in the object. Suitable light-houses on the most dangerous points, would annually save, from otherwise inevitable destruction, many vessels and preserve hundreds of valuable lives. The profession of these marauders would be, in such a case, but a sinecure; provided they would allow the lights to remain. But, unless each tower were converted into a well-manned gun-battery the piratical character of these men will preclude any hope of their permanent establishment. Men of their buccaneering habits are not likely to lie quietly on their oars, and see their means of livelihood torn from them by the secure navigation of these waters. They will sound, from island to island, the tocsin for the gathering of their strength, and concentrate for the destruction of these enemies to their *honest calling*, before they have cast their cheering beams over these stormy seas a score of nights.

As we approached the Hole in the Wall, the breeze which we had brought down the channel, stole in advance and set in motion the fleet of becalmed vessels, which rolled heavily on the long, ground-swell, about a league ahead of us. The spur or promontory of Abaco, around which we were sailing, is a high, wall-like ridge of rock, whose surface gradually inclines from the main body of the island to its abrupt termination about a quarter of a league into the sea. As we sailed along its eastern side we could not detect the opening from which it derives its name. The eye met only a long black wall of rock, whose rugged projections were hung with festoons of dark purple sea-weed, and around whose base the waters surged, with a roar heard distinctly by us, three miles from the island.

On rounding the extremity of the head-land, and bearing up a point or two, the arch in the Cape gradually opened till it became wholly visible, apparently about half the altitude of, and very similar in appearance to the Natural bridge in Virginia. The chasm is irregularly arched, and broader at thirty feet from the sea than at its base. The water is of sufficient depth, and the arch lofty enough, to allow small fishing vessels to pass through the aperture, which is about one hundred feet in length through the solid rock. There is a gap which would indicate the former existence of a similar cavity, near the end of this head-land. A large, isolated mass of rock is here detached from the main wall, at its termination in the sea, which was undoubtedly, at some former period, joined to it by a natural arch, now fallen into the water, as, probably, will happen to this within a century.

These cavities are caused by the undermining of the sea, which, dashing unceasingly against the foundations of the wall, shatters and crumbles it by its constant abrasion, opens through it immense fissures, and loosens large fragments of the rock, that easily yield and give way to its increased violence; while the upper stratum, high beyond the reach of the surge, remains firm, and, long after the base has crumbled into the sea, arches over like a bridge the chasm beneath. By and by this falls by its own weight, and is buried beneath the waves.

As the shades of night fell over the sea, and veiled the land from our eyes, we had a fresh object of excitement in giving chase to the vessels which, as the sun went down among them, were scattered thickly along the western horizon far ahead of us—ships, brigs, and schooners, stretching away under all sail before the evening breeze to the south and west. We had lost sight of them after night had set in, but at about half past eight in the evening, as we all were peering through the darkness, upon the *qui vive* for the strangers, a bright light flashed upon our eyes over the water, and at the same moment the lookout forward electrified us with the cry— —

"A ship dead ahead, sir!"

The captain seized his speaking-trumpet, and sprang to the bows; but we were there before him, and discovered a solitary light burning at the base of a dark pyramid, which towered gloomily in the obscurity of the night. The outline of the object was so confused and blended with the sky, that we could discern it but indistinctly. To our optics it appeared, as it loomed up in the night-haze, to be a ship of the largest class. The spy glass was in immediate requisition, but soon laid aside again.

Let me inform you that "day and night" marked upon the tube of a spy-glass, signifies that it may be used in the day, and kept in the beckets at night.

We had been gathered upon the bowsprit and forecastle but a few seconds, watching in silence the dark moving tower on the water before us, as we approached it rapidly, when we were startled by the sudden hail of the stranger, who was now hauling up on our weather bow—

"Ship-ahoy!" burst loudly over the water from the hoarse throat of a trumpet.

"Ahoy!" bellowed our captain, so gently back again through the ship's trumpet, that the best "bull of Bashan" might have envied him his roar.

"What ship's that?"

"The Plato of Portland," with a second bellow which was a very manifest improvement upon the preceding.

"Where bound?"

"New-Orleans!"

Now came our turn to play the querist. "What ship's that?"

"The J. L., eleven days from New-York, bound to New-Orleans."

"Ay, ay—any news?"

"No, nothing particular."

We again moved on in silence; sailing in company, but not always in sight of each other, during the remainder of the night.

A delightful prospect met our eyes, on coming on deck the morning after making the Hole in the Wall. The sea was crowded with vessels, bearing upon its silvery bosom a floating city. By some fortuitous circumstance, a fleet of vessels, bearing the flags of various nations, had arrived in the Bahama channel at the same time, and now, were amicably sailing in company, borne by the same waves—wafted by the same breeze, and standing toward the same point. Our New-York friend, for whom, on casting our eyes over the lively scene we first searched, we discovered nearly two leagues from us to the windward, stretching boldly across the most dangerous part of the Bahama Banks, instead of taking, with the rest of the fleet, the farther but less hazardous course down the "Channel"—if a few inches more of water than the Banks are elsewhere covered with, may with propriety be thus denominated.

A little to the south of us, rocking upon the scarcely rising billows, was a rough clumsy looking craft, with one low, black mast, and amputated bowsprit, about four feet in length, sustaining a jib of no particular hue or dimensions. Hoisted upon the mast, was extended a dark red painted mainsail, blackened by the smoke, which, issuing from a black wooden chimney amidships, curled gracefully upward and floated away on the breeze in thin blue clouds. A little triangular bit of red bunting fluttered at her mast head; and, towed by a long line at her stern, a little green whale-boat skipped and danced merrily over the waves. Standing, or rather reclining at the helm—for men learn strangely indolent postures in the warm south—with a segar between his lips, and his eye fixed earnestly upon the J. L., was a black-whiskered fellow, whose head was enveloped in a tri-coloured, conical cap, terminated by a tassel, which dangled over his left ear. A blue flannel shirt, and white flowing trowsers, with which his body and limbs were covered, were secured to his person by a red sash tied around the waist, instead of suspenders. Two others similarly dressed, and as bountifully bewhiskered, leaned listlessly over the side gazing at our ship, as she dashed proudly past their rude bark. A negro, whose charms would have been unquestionable in Congo, was stretched, apparently asleep, along the main-boom, which one moment swung with him over the water, and the next suspended him over his chimney, whose azure incense ascended from his own altar, to this ebony deity, in clouds of grateful odour.

"What craft do you call that?" inquired one of the passengers of the captain.

"What? It's a wrecker's lugger.—Watch him now!"

At the moment he spoke, the lugger dropped astern of us, came to a few points—hauled close on the wind, and then gathering headway, bounded off with the speed of the wind in the direction of the New-York packet ship, which the wrecker's quicker and more practised eye had detected displaying signals of distress. Turning our glasses in the direction of the ship, we could see that she had grounded on the bank, thereby affording very ample illustration of the truth of the proverb, "The more haste the less speed."

About the middle of the forenoon the wind died away, and left us becalmed within half a mile of a brig loaded with lumber. The remaining vessels of the fleet were fast dispersing over the sea—this Yankee "fruiterer" being the only one sailing within a league of us.

These lumber vessels, which are usually loaded with shingles, masts, spars, and boards, have been long the floating mines of Maine. But as her forests disappear, which are the veins from whence she draws the ore, her sons will have to plough the earth instead of the ocean. Then, and not till then, will Maine take a high rank as an agricultural state. The majority of men who sail in these lumber vessels are both farmers and sailors; who cultivate their farms at one season, fell its timber and sail away with it in the shape of boards and shingles to a West India mart at another. Jonathan is the only man who knows how to carry on two trades at one time, and carry them on successfully.

For their lumber, which they more frequently *barter* away than sell, they generally obtain a return cargo of molasses, which is converted by our "sober and moral" fellow-countrymen into liquid gunpowder, in the vats of those numerous distilleries, which, like guide-posts to the regions of death, line the sea skirts of New-England!

The smooth bottom, above which we were suspended, through the deceptive transparency of the water, appeared, though eighteen feet beneath us, within reach of the oar. But there were many objects floating by upon the surface, which afforded us more interest than all beneath it.

Among these was the little nautilus which, gaily dancing over the waves, like a Lilliputian mariner,

> "Spreads his thin oar and courts the rising gale."

This beautiful animal sailed past us in fleets wafted by a breeze gentler than an infant's breathing. We endeavoured to secure one of them more beautiful than its fellows, but like a sensitive plant it instantly shrunk at the touch, and sunk beneath the surface; appearing beneath the water, like a little, animated globule tinged with the most delicate colours. This singular animal is termed by the sailors, "The Portuguee' man-o'-war," from what imaginary resemblance to the war vessels of His Most Christian Majesty I am at a loss to determine; unless we resort for a solution of the mystery to a jack-tar, whom I questioned upon the subject—

"It's cause as how they takes in all sail, or goes *chuck* to bottom, when it 'gins to blow a spankin' breeze,"—truly a fine compliment to the navarchy of Portugal!

This animal is a genus of the mollusca tribe, which glitters in the night on the crest of every bursting wave. In the tropical seas it is found riding over the gently ruffled billows in great numbers, with its crystalline sail expanded to the light breeze—barks delicate and tiny enough for fairy "Queen Mab." Termed by naturalists *pharsalia,* from its habit of inflating its transparent sail, this splendid animal is often confounded with the *nautilus pompilius,* a genus of marine animals of an entirely distinct species, and of a much ruder appearance, whose dead shells are found floating every where in the tropical seas, while the living animal is found swimming upon the ocean in every latitude.

Dr. Coates, in describing the Portuguese man-of-war (pharsalia) says, that "it is an oblong animated sack of air, elongated at one extremity into a conical neck, and surmounted by a membraneous expansion running nearly the whole length of the body, and rising above into a semi-circular sail, which can be expanded or contracted to a considerable extent at the pleasure of the animal. From beneath the body are suspended from ten to fifty, or more little tubes, from half an inch to an inch in length, open at their lower extremity, and formed like the flower of the blue bottle. These I cannot but consider as proper stomachs, from the centre of which depends a little cord, never exceeding the fourth of an inch in thickness, and often forty times as long as the body.

"The group of stomachs is less transparent, and although the hue is the same as that of the back, they are on this account incomparably less elegant. By their weight and form they fill the double office of a keel and ballast, while the cord-like appendage, which floats out for yards behind, is called by seamen "the cable." With this organ, which is supposed by naturalists, from the extreme pain felt, when brought in contact with the back of the hand, to secrete a poisonous or acrid fluid, the animal secures his prey." But in the opinion of Dr. C. naturalists in deciding upon this mere hypothesis have concluded too hastily. He says that the secret will be better explained by a more careful examination of the organ itself. "The cord is composed of a narrow layer of contractile fibres, scarcely visible when relaxed, on account of its transparency. If the animal be large, this layer of fibres will sometimes extend itself to the length of four or five yards. A spiral line of blue, bead-like bodies, less than the head of a pin, revolves around the cable from end to end, and under the microscope these beads appear covered with minute prickles so hard and sharp that they will readily enter the substance of wood, adhering with such pertinacity that the cord can rarely be detached without breaking.

"It is to these prickles that the man-of-war owes its power of destroying animals much its superior in strength and activity. When any thing becomes impaled upon the cords, the contractile fibres are called into action, and rapidly shrink from many feet in length to less than the same number of inches, bringing the prey within reach of the little tubes, by one of which it is immediately swallowed.

"Its size varies from half an inch to six inches in length. When it is in motion the sail is accommodated to the force of the breeze, and the elongated neck is curved upward, giving to the animal a form strongly resembling the little glass swans which we sometimes see swimming in goblets.

"It is not the form, however, which constitutes the chief beauty of this little navigator. The lower part of the body and the neck are devoid of all colours except a faint iridescence in reflected lights, and they are so perfectly transparent that the finest print is not obscured when viewed through them. The back becomes gradually tinged as we ascend, with the finest and most delicate hues that can be imagined; the base of the sail equals the purest sky in depth and beauty of tint; the summit is of the most splendid red, and the central part is shaded by the gradual intermixture of these colours through all the intermediate grades of purple. Drawn as it were upon a ground-work of mist, the tints have an aerial softness far beyond the reach of art."

V

During the period we lay becalmed under a burning sun, which, though entering its winter solstice retained the fervour of summer fire, we passed the most of our time in the little cockle-shell of a yawl, (as though the limits of our ship were not confined enough) riding listlessly upon the long billows or rowing far out from the ship, which, with all her light sails furled, rolled heavily upon the crestless billows, suggesting the anomalous idea of power in a state of helplessness.

An hour before sunset our long-idle sails were once more filled by a fine breeze, which, ruffling the surface of the ocean more than a league distant, we had discerned coming from the Florida shore, some time before it reached us; and as it came slowly onward over the sea, we watched with no little anxiety the agitated line of waves which danced merrily before it, marking its approach.

A faintly delineated gray bank lining the western horizon, marked the "land of flowers" of the romantic Ponce de Leon. Can that be Florida! the *Pasqua de Flores* of the Spaniards—the country of blossoms and living fountains, welling with perpetual youth! were our reflections as we gazed upon the low marshy shore. Yet here the avaricious Spaniard sought for a mine more precious than the diamonds and gold of the Incas! a fountain whose waters were represented to have the wonderful property of rejuvenating old age and perpetuating youth! Here every wrinkled Castilian Iolas expected to find a Hebé to restore him to the bloom and vigour of Adonis! But alas, for the bachelors of modern days, the seeker for fountains of eternal youth wandered only through inhospitable wilds, and encountered the warlike Seminoles, who, unlike the timorous natives of the newly discovered Indies, met his little band with bold and determined resolution. After a long and fruitless search, he returned to Porto Rico, wearied, disappointed, and no doubt with his brow more deeply furrowed than when he set out upon his singularly romantic expedition.

While we glided along the Florida shore, which was fast receding from the eye, a sudden boiling and commotion of the sea, which we had remarked some time before we were involved in it, assured us that we had again entered the Gulf Stream, where it rushes from the Mexican Sea, after having made a broad sweep of eighteen hundred miles, and in twenty days after emerging from it in higher latitudes. Our course was now very sensibly retarded by the strong current against which we sailed, though impelled by a breeze which would have wafted us, over a currentless sea, nine or ten miles an hour. In the afternoon the blue hills of Cuba, elevated above the undulating surface of the island, and stretching along its back like a serrated spine, reared themselves from the sea far to the south; and at sunset the twin hills of Matanzas, for which sailors' imaginations have conjured up not the most pleasing appellation—could be just distinguished from the blue waves on the verge of the ocean; and receding from the sea, with an uneven surface, the vast island rose along the whole southern horizon, not more than four or five leagues distant. The Florida shore had long before disappeared, though several vessels were standing toward it, bound apparently into Key West, between which and Havana we had seen an armed schooner, under American colours, hovering during the whole afternoon.

Cape St. Antonio, the notorious rendezvous of that daring band of pirates, which, possessing the marauding without the chivalrous spirit of the old buccaneers, long infested these seas, just protruded above the rim of the horizon far to the south-east. We soon lost sight of it, and in the evening, altering our course a little to avoid the shoals which are scattered thickly off the southern and western extremity of Florida, ran rapidly and safely past the Tortugas—the Scylla and Charybdis of this southern latitude.

We already begin to appreciate the genial influence of a southern climate. The sun, tempered by a pleasant wind, beams down upon us warm and cheerily—the air is balmy and laden with grateful fragrance from the unseen land—and though near the first of December, at which time you dwellers under the wintry skies of the north, are shivering over your grates, we have worn our summer garments and palm-leaf hats for some days past. If this is a specimen of a southern winter, where quietly to inhale the mellow air is an elysian enjoyment—henceforth sleighing and skating will have less charms for me.

We are at last at the termination of our voyage upon the *sea*. In three days at the farthest we expect to land in New-Orleans. But three days upon the waveless Mississippi to those who have been riding a month upon the ocean, is but a trifle. After an uncommonly long, but unusually pleasant passage of thirty-one days, we anchored off the Balize[1] last evening at sun set.

The tedious monotony of our passage since leaving Cuba, was more than cancelled by the scenes and variety of yesterday. We had not seen a sail for four or five days, when, on ascending to the deck at sunrise yesterday morning, judge of my surprise and pleasure at beholding a fleet of nearly fifty vessels surrounding us on every side, all standing to one common centre; in the midst of which our own gallant ship dashed proudly on, like a high mettled courser contending for the victory. To one imprisoned in a companionless ship on the broad and lonely ocean so many days, this was a scene, from its vivid contrast, calculated to awaken in the bosom emotions of the liveliest gratification and pleasure.

A point or two abaft our beam, within pistol shot distance, slowly and majestically moved a huge, British West Indiaman, her black gloomy hull wholly unrelieved by brighter colours, with her red ensign heavily unfolding to the breeze in recognition of the stars and stripes, floating gracefully at our peak. Farther astern, a taunt-rigged, rakish looking Portuguese polacca (polaque) carrying even in so light a breeze a "bone in her teeth," glided swiftly along, every thing set from deck to truck. We could distinctly see the red woollen caps and dark red faces of her crew, peering over the bow, as they pointed to, and made remarks upon our ship. Early in the morning, about a league ahead of us, we had observed a heavy sailing Dutch ship, as indeed all Dutch ships are; about eleven o'clock we came up with, and passed her, with the same facility as if she had been at anchor. On all sides of us vessels of nearly every maritime nation were in sight; and in conjectures respecting them, and in admiring their variety of construction and appearance, we passed most of the day, elated with the prospect of a speedy termination to our voyage.

Before we had completed dinner, the cry of "Land ho!" was heard from the main-top, and in the course of half an hour we saw from the deck, not exactly *land*, but an apology for it, in the form and substance of an immense marsh of tall, wild grass, which stretched along the horizon from west to east *ad infinitum*. This soil, if you may term it such, is formed by the accumulation and deposition of ochreous matter discharged by the Mississippi, whose turbid waters are more or less charged with terrene particles, so much so, that a glass filled with its water appears to deposit in a short time a sediment nearly equal to one-twelfth of its bulk. The matter discharged by the river, condensed and strengthened by logs, trees, grass, and other gross substances, is raised above the ordinary tide waters, upon which a soil is formed of mingled sand and marl, capable of producing the long grass, which not only lines the coast in the vicinity of this river, but extends many miles into the interior, where it unites with the cypress swamps which cover the greater part of the unreclaimed lowlands of Louisiana. We coasted along this shore till about three in the afternoon, when the light-house at the South-East passage, the chief *embouchure* of the Mississippi, appeared in sight but a few miles ahead; passing this, we received a pilot from a fairy-like pilot-boat, which, on delivering him, bounded away from us like a swift-winged albatross. About four o'clock the light-house at the South-West passage lifted its solitary head above the horizon. The breeze freshening, we approached it rapidly, under the guidance of the pilot, who had taken command of our ship. When nearly abreast of the light-house, a fierce little warlike-looking revenue cutter ran alongside of us, and lowering her boat, sent her lieutenant on board, to see that "all was straight." He cracked a bottle of wine with the captain, and leaving some late New-Orleans papers, took his departure. For the next half hour the quarter-deck appeared like a school-room—buzz, buzz, buzz! till the papers were read and re-read, advertisements and all, and all were satisfied. About six in the evening we cast anchor at the mouth of the South-West pass, in company not only with the fleet in which we had sailed during the day, but with a large fleet already at anchor, waiting for tide, pilots, wind, or tow-boats. In approaching the mouth of the river, we observed, to us, a novel and remarkable appearance—the meeting of the milky, turbid waters of the Mississippi, with the pale green of the ocean. The waters of the former, being lighter than the latter, and not readily mingling with it, are thrown upon the surface, floating like oil to the depth of only two or three feet. A ship passing through this water, leaves a long, dark wake, which is slowly covered by the uniting of the parted waters. The line of demarkation between the yellowish-brown water of the river, and the clear green water of the sea, is so distinctly defined, that a cane could be laid along it. When we first discovered the long white line, about two miles distant, it presented the appearance of a low sand beach. As we reached it, I went aloft, and seating myself in the top-gallant cross-trees, beheld one of the most singular appearances of which I had ever formed any conception. When within a few fathoms of the discoloured water, we appeared to be rushing on to certain destruction, and when our sharp keel cut and turned up the sluggish surface, I involuntarily shuddered; the next instant we seemed suspended between two seas. Another moment, and we had passed the line of division, ploughing the lazy and muddy waves, and leaving a dark transparent wake far astern. We are hourly expecting our tow-boat—the Whale. When she arrives we shall immediately, in the company of some other ships, move up for New-Orleans. The morning is delightful, and we have the prospect of a pleasant sail, or rather *tow*, up the river. A hundred snow-white sails are reflecting the rays of the morning sun, while the rapid dashing of the swift pilot-boats about us, and the slower movements of ships getting under weigh to cross the bar, and work their own way up to the city—together with the mingling sounds of stern commands, and the sonorous "heave-ho-yeo!" of the labouring seamen, borne upon the breeze, give an almost unparalleled charm and novelty to the scene. Our Whale is now in sight, spouting, not *jets d'eau*, but volumes of dense black smoke. We shall soon be under weigh, and every countenance is bright with anticipation. Within an hour we shall be floating upon the great artery of North America, "prisoners of hope" and of *steam*, on our way to add our little number to the countless thousands who throng the streets of the Key of the Great Valley through which it flows.

FOOTNOTE

[1] French balise, Spanish, valiza, a *beacon*; once placed at the mouth of the river, but now superseded by a light-house. Hence the term "Balize" applied to the mouth of the Mississippi.

PART II

V

Upon the mighty bosom of the "Father of Waters", our gallant ship now proudly floats. The Mississippi! that noble river, whose magnificent windings I have traced with my finger upon the map in my school-boy days, wishing, with all the adventurous longing of a boy, that I might, like the good fathers Marquette and Hennepin, leap into an Indian's birch canoe, and launching from its source among the snows and untrodden wilds of the far north, float pleasantly away under every climate, down to the cis-Atlantic Mediterranean; where, bursting from its confined limits, it proudly shoots into that tideless sea through numerous passages, like radii from one common centre. My wishes are now, in a measure, about to be realized. The low, flat, and interminable marshes, through the heart of which we are rapidly advancing—the ocean-like horizon, unrelieved by the slightest prominence—the sullen, turbid waves around us, which yield but slowly and heavily to the irresistible power of steam—all familiar characteristics of this river—would alone assure me that I am on the Mississippi. My last letter left us in the immediate expectation of being taken in tow by the "Whale," then coming rapidly down the South-West passage, in obedience to the hundred signals flying at the "fore" of as many vessels on every side of us. In a few minutes, snorting and dashing over the long ground-swell, and flinging a cloud of foam from her bows, she ran alongside of us, and sent her boat on board. While the little skiff was leaping from wave to wave to our ship, we had time to observe more attentively than when in motion, the singular appearance of this *unique* class of steamboats.

Her engine is of uncommon power, placed nearer the centre of the hull than in boats of the usual construction; her cabin is small, elevated, and placed near the engine in the centre of the boat. With the exception of the engine and cabin, she is "flush" from stem to stern; one quarter of her length abaft the cabin, and the same portion forward of the boilers being a broad platform, which extends quite around the boat, forming a very spacious guard on either side.

The after part of this guard is latticed for the purpose of carrying off the water with facility when thrown back from the wheels. They seldom or never take passengers up to the city. The usual price for towing is, I think, about one dollar *per* ton. Hence the expense is very great for vessels of large burthen; and rather than incur it, many ships, after being towed over the bar, which, at this season, cannot be crossed otherwise, work their own way up to town, which, with a fair wind, may be effected in twenty-four hours, the distance being but one hundred and five miles; but it not unfrequently takes them ten or fifteen days. Our captain informs me that he once lay thirty-six days in the river before he could reach New-Orleans—but fortunately, owing to the state of the market, on his arrival, he realized two hundred per cent. more on his cargo than he would have done had he arrived a month earlier.

The jolly-boat from the steamer was now along side, and the officer in the stern sheets tossed a small package on our quarter-deck; and then, with the velocity of an uncaged bird, his little green cockle-shell darted away from us like a dolphin. The next moment he stood upon the low deck of the steamer.

"Go ahead!" loudly was borne over the water, and with a plunge and a struggle, away she dashed from us with her loud, regular *boom, boom, boom*! throwing the spray around her head, like the huge gambolling monster from which she derives her name. With her went our hopes of speedy deliverance from our present durance. With faces whose complicated, whimsically-woful expression Lavater himself could not have analyzed, and as though moved by one spirit, we turned simultaneously toward the captain, who leaned against the capstan, reading one of the letters from the package just received. There was a cloud upon his brow which portended no good to our hopes, and which, by a sympathetic feeling, was attracted to, and heavily settled upon our own. We turned simultaneously to the tow-boat: she was rapidly receding in the distance. We turned again to watch our probable fate in the captain's face. It spoke as plainly as face could speak, "gentlemen, *no* tow-boat." We gazed upon each other like school-boys hatching a conspiracy. Mutual glances of chagrin and dissatisfaction were bandied about the decks. After so long a passage, with our port almost in sight, and our voyage nearly ended, to be compelled to remain longer in our close prison, and creep like a

"Wounded snake, dragging its slow length along,"

winding, day after day, through the sinuosities of this sluggish Mississippi, was enough to make us ship-wearied wretches verily,

"To weep our spirits from our eyes."

It was a consummation we had never wished. There was evidently a rebellion in embryo. The storm was rapidly gathering, and the thunders had already begun "to utter their voices." The whole scene was infinitely amusing. There could not have been more *feeling* exhibited, had an order come down for the ship to ride a Gibraltar quarantine.

The captain, having quietly finished the perusal of his letters, now changed at once the complexion of affairs.

"I have just received advices, gentlemen, from my consignees in the city, that the market will be more favourable for my cargo fifteen days hence, than now; therefore, as I have so much leisure before me, I shall decline taking the tow-boat, and sail up to New-Orleans. I will, however, send my boat aboard the brig off our starboard quarter, which will take steam, and try to engage passage for those who wish to leave the ship."

There was no alternative, and we cheerfully sacrificed our individual wishes to the interests of Captain Callighan, whose urbanity, kindness and gentlemanly deportment, during the whole passage out, had not only contributed to our comfort and happiness, but won for him our cordial esteem and good feelings.[2]

In a few minutes one of our quarter-boats was alongside, bobbing up and down on the short seas, with the buoyancy of a cork-float. The first officer, myself, and another passenger, leaped into her; and a few dozen long and nervous strokes from the muscular arms of our men, soon ran us aboard the brig, whose anchor was already "apeak," in readiness for the Whale. As we approached her, I was struck with her admirable symmetry and fine proportions—she was a perfect model of naval architecture. Though rather long for her breadth of beam, the sharp construction of her bows, and the easy, elliptical curve of her sides, gave her a peculiarly light and graceful appearance, which, united with her taunt, slightly raking taper masts, and the precision of her rigging, presented to our view a nautical *ensemble*, surpassing in elegance any thing of the kind I had ever before beheld.

We were politely received at the gangway by the captain, a gentlemanly, sailor-like looking young man, with whom, after introducing ourselves, we descended into the cabin. I had time, however, to notice that the interior of this very handsome vessel corresponded with the exterior. The capstan, the quarter-rail stanchions, the edge of the companion-way, and the taffrail, were all ornamented and strengthened with massive brass plates, polished like a mirror. The binnacle case was of ebony, enriched with inlaying and carved work. A dazzling array of steel-headed boarding pikes formed a glittering crescent half around the main-mast. Her decks evinced the free use of the "holy-stone," and in snowy whiteness, would have put to the blush the unsoiled floors of the most fastidious Yankee housewife. Her rigging was not hung on pins, but run and coiled "man-o'-war fashion," upon her decks. Her long boat, amidships, was rather an ornament than an excrescence, as in most merchantmen. Forward, the "men" were gathered around the windlass, which was abaft the foremast, all neatly dressed in white trousers and shirts, even to the sable "Doctor" and his "sub," whose double banks of ivories were wonderingly illuminative, as they grinned at the strangers who had so unceremoniously boarded the brig.

As I descended the mahogany stair-case, supported by a highly polished balustrade cast in brass, my curiosity began to be roused, and I found myself wondering into what pleasure-yacht I had intruded. She was evidently American; for the "stars and stripes" were floating over our heads. Independent of this evidence of her nation, her bright, golden sides, and peculiar American *expression* (for I contend that there is a national and an individual expression to every vessel, as strongly marked and as easily defined as the expression of every human countenance,) unhesitatingly indicated her country.

My curiosity was increased on entering the roomy, richly wrought, and tastefully furnished cabin. The fairest lady in England's halls might have coveted it for her *boudoir*. Here were every luxury and comfort, that wealth and taste combined could procure. A piano, on which lay music books, a flute, clarionet, and a guitar of curious workmanship, occupied one side of the cabin; on the other stood a sofa, most temptingly inviting a loll, and a centre table was strewed with pamphlets, novels, periodicals, poetry, and a hundred little unwritten elegancies. The transom was ingeniously constructed, so as to form a superb sideboard, richly covered with plate, but more richly *lined*, as we subsequently had an opportunity of knowing, to our hearts' content. Three doors with mirrored panelling gave egress from the cabin, forward, to two state rooms and a dining-room, furnished in the same style of magnificence.

My companions shared equally in my surprise, at the novelty of every thing around us. I felt a disposition to return to our ship, fearing that our proposition to take passage in the brig might be unacceptable. But before I had come to a decision, Mr. F., our first officer, with true sailor-like bluntness, had communicated our situation and wishes. "Certainly," replied the captain, "but I regret that my state-rooms will not accommodate more than five or six; the others will have to swing hammocks between decks; if they will do this, they are welcome." Although this compliance with our request was given with the utmost cheerfulness and alacrity, I felt that our taking passage with him would be inconvenient and a gross intrusion; and would have declined saying, that some other vessel would answer our purpose equally well. He would not listen to me but in so urgent a manner requested us to take passage with him, that we reluctantly consented, and immediately returned to our ship to relate our success, and transfer our baggage to the brig. Fortunately, but five of our party, including two ladies, were anxious to leave the ship; the remainder choosing rather to remain on board, and go up to town in her, as the captain flattered them with the promise of an early arrival should the wind hold fair.

In less than ten minutes we had bidden farewell, and wished a speedy passage to our fellow-passengers, who had so rashly refused to "give up the ship" and were on our way with "bag and baggage" to the brig, which now and then rose proudly upon a long sea, and then slowly and gracefully settled into its yielding bosom.

We had been on board but a short time when the Whale, which had already towed four ships and a brig, one at a time, over the bar, leaving each half a league up the passage, came bearing down upon us. In an incredibly short time she brought to ahead of us, and in less than five minutes had our brig firmly secured to her by two hawsers, with about fifty fathoms play.

In the course of half an hour, we arrived where the five other vessels, which were to accompany us in tow, were anchored. More than two hours were consumed in properly securing the vessels to the tow-boat. Our brig was lashed to her larboard, and the huge British Indiaman, mentioned in my last letter, to her starboard side. Two ships sociably followed, about a cable's length astern, and a Spanish brig and a French ship, about one hundred yards astern of these, brought up the rear.

These arrangements completed, the command to "go ahead" was given, and slowly, one after the other, the captive fleet yielded to the immense power of the high-pressure engine. Gradually our motion through the water became more and more rapid, till we moved along at the rate of seven knots an hour. The appearance our convoy presented, was novel and sublime. It was like a triumph! The wind though light, was fair, and every vessel was covered with clouds of snowy canvass. The loud, deep, incessant booming from the tow-boat—the black and dense masses of smoke rolling up and curling and wreathing around the lofty white sails, then shooting off horizontally through the air, leaving a long cloudy galaxy astern, contributed greatly to the novelty of this extraordinary scene. We are now within twenty miles of the city of Frenchmen and garlic soups, steamboats and yellow fever, negroes and quadroons, hells and convents, soldiers and slaves, and things, and people of every language and kindred, nation and tribe upon the face of the earth. From this place you will receive my next letter, wherein perchance you may find a solution of the mystery thrown around our beautiful vessel.

FOOTNOTE

[2] Our ship was not a line-packet: they never delay.

VII.

We are at last in New-Orleans, the queen of the South-west—the American Waterloo, whose Wellington, "General Jackson"—according to the elegant ballad I believe still extant in the "Boston picture-books,"

—— "quick did go
With Yankee(?) troops to meet the foe;
We met them near to New-Orleans
And made their blood to flow in streams."

New-Orleans! the play-thing of monarchs. "Swapped," as boys swap their penknives. Discovered and lost by the French—possessed by the gold-hunting Spaniard—again ceded to the French—exchanged for a kingdom with the man who traded in empires, and sold by him, for a "plum" to our government!

We arrived between eight and nine last evening, after a very pleasant run of twenty-eight hours from the Balize, charmed and delighted of course with every thing. If we had landed at the entrance of Vulcan's smithy from so long a sea-passage, it would have been precisely the same—all would have appeared *"couleur de rose."* To be *on land*, even were it a sand bank, is all that is requisite to render it in the eyes of the new landed passenger, a Paradise.

During the first part of our sail up the river, there was nothing sufficiently interesting in the way of incident or variety of scenery, to merit the trouble either of narration or perusal. Till we arrived within forty-five or fifty miles of New-Orleans, the shores of the river presented the same flat, marshy appearance previously described. With the exception of two or three "pilot stations," near its mouth, I do not recollect that we passed any dwelling. These "stations" are situated within a few miles of the mouth of the river, and are the residences of the pilots. The one on the left bank of the river, which I had an opportunity of visiting, contained about sixteen or eighteen houses, built upon piles, in the midst of the morass, which is the only apology for land within twenty leagues. One third of these are dwelling houses, connected with each other for the purpose of intercourse, by raised walks or bridges, laid upon the surface of the mud, and constructed of timber, logs, and wrecks of vessels. Were a hapless wight to lose his footing, he would descend as easily and gracefully into the bosom of the yielding loam, as into a barrel of soft soap. The intercourse with the shore, near which this miserable, isolated congregation of shanties is imbedded, is also kept up by a causeway of similar construction and materials.

The pilots, of whom there are from twelve to twenty at each station, are a hardy, rugged class of men. Most of them have been mates of merchantmen, or held some inferior official station in the navy. The majority of them, I believe, are English, though Americans, Frenchmen and Spaniards, are not wanting among their number. The moral character of this class of men, generally, does not stand very high, though there are numerous instances of individuals among them, whose nautical skill and gentlemanly deportment reflect honour upon their profession.

It is by no means an unusual circumstance for the commander of a ship, on entering a harbour, to resign, *pro tem.*, the charge of his vessel to a pilot, whom a few years before, while a petty officer under his command, he may have publicly disgraced and dismissed from his ship for some misdemeanor.

In eighteen hundred and twenty-seven, when off Maldonado, ascending the La Plata, a Spanish pilot came on board a ship of war; and as he stalked aft from the gangway, with the assumed hauteur of littleness in power, the penetrating eye of one of the lieutenants was fixed upon his countenance with a close and scrutinizing gaze. The eye of the pilot fell beneath its stern expression for a moment; but he again raised it, and stealing a quick, furtive, and apparently recognising glance at the officer, his dark brown face changed suddenly to the hue of death, and with a fearful cry, he sprang with the activity of a cat into the mizen rigging; but before he could leap over the quarter, the officer had seized a musket from a marine, and fired: the ball struck him near the elbow the instant he had cleared the rigging. A heavy splash was heard in the water, and as those on deck flew to the stern, a dark spot of blood upon the water was the only evidence that a human being had sunk beneath. While they were engaged in looking upon the spot where he had plunged, and wondering, without knowing the cause, at this summary method of proceeding on the part of the lieutenant, a cry, "there he is," was heard and repeated by fifty voices, naval discipline to the contrary notwithstanding, and about twenty fathoms astern, the black head of the pilot was seen emerging from the waves—but the next instant, with a horrible Spanish curse, he dived fròm their sight, and in a few minutes, appeared more than a hundred yards astern.

It appeared that during the well-known piratical depredations, a few years previous, in the vicinity of Key West and Cape St. Antonio, this officer had the command of a shore expedition against the pirates. During the excursion he attacked a large band of them in their retreats, and, after a long and warmly contested conflict, either slew or took the whole party prisoners. Among those was the redoubtable pilot, who held the goodly office of second in command among those worthy gentlemen. But as they proceeded to their schooner, which lay half a league from the shore, the rover, not liking the prospect which his skill in "second sight" presented to his fancy, suddenly, with a powerful effort, threw off the two men between whom he was seated, and leaping, with both arms pinioned behind him, over the head of the astonished bow oarsman, disappeared "instanter;" and while a score of muskets and pistols were levelled in various directions, made his appearance, in a few minutes, about a furlong astern, and out of reach of shot. It was thought useless to pursue him in a heavy barge, and he effected his escape. This said swimmer was recognised by the lieutenant in the person of the pilot; and as the recognition was mutual, the scene I have narrated followed.

At sunrise, the morning after leaving the Balize, we passed the ruins, or rather the former location, (for the traces are scarcely perceptible) of the old Spanish fort Plaquemine, where, while this country was under Spanish government, all vessels were obliged to heave to, and produce their passports for the inspection of the sage, big-whiskered Dons, who were there whilom domesticated.

Toward noon, the perpetual sameness of the shores, (they cannot be termed *banks*) of the river, were relieved by clumps of cypress and other trees, which gradually, as we advanced, increased into forests, extending back to a level horizon, as viewed from the mast-head, and overhanging both sides of the river. Though so late in the season, they still retained the green freshness of summer, and afforded an agreeable contrast to the dry and leafless forests which we had just left at the north. At a distance, we beheld the first plantation to be seen on ascending the river. As we approached it, we discovered from the deck the commencement of the embankment or "Levée," which extends, on both sides of the river, to more than one hundred and fifty miles above New-Orleans. This *levée* is properly a dike, thrown up on the verge of the river, from twenty-five to thirty feet in breadth, and two feet higher than high-water mark; leaving a ditch, or fossé, on the inner side, of equal breadth, from which the earth to form the levée is taken. Consequently, as the land bordering on the river is a dead level, and, without the security of the levée, overflowed at half tides, when the river is full, or within twenty inches, as it often is, of the top of the embankment, the surface of the river will be *four feet higher* than the surface of the country; the altitude of the inner side of the levée being usually six feet above the general surface of the surrounding land.

This is a startling truth; and at first leads to reflections by no means favorable in their results, to the safety, either of the lives or property of the inhabitants of the lowlands of Louisiana. But closer observation affords the assurance that however threatening a mass of water four feet in height, two thousand five hundred in breadth, and of infinite length, may be in appearance, experience has not shown to any great extent, that the residents on the borders of this river have in reality, more to apprehend from an inundation, so firm and efficacious is their levée, than those who reside in more apparent security, upon the elevated banks of our flooding rivers of the north. It cannot be denied that there have been instances where "crevasses" as they are termed here, have been gradually worn through the levée, by the attrition of the waters, when, suddenly starting through in a wiry stream, they rapidly enlarge to torrents which, with the force, and noise, and rushing of a mill-race, shoot away over the plantations, inundating the sugar fields, and losing themselves in the boundless marshes in the rear. But on such occasions, which however are not frequent, the alarm is given and communicated by the plantation bells, and before half an hour elapses, several hundred negroes, with their masters, (who all turn out on these occasions, as at a fire,) will have gathered to the spot, and at the expiration of another half-hour, the breach will be stopped, the danger past, and the "Monarch of rivers," subdued by the hand of man, will be seen again moving, submissively obedient, within his prescribed limits, sullenly, yet majestically to the ocean.

During the afternoon, we passed successively many sugar plantations, in the highest state of cultivation. Owing to the elevation of the levée, and the low situation of the lands, we could see from the deck only the upper story of the planters' residences upon the shore; but from the main top, we had an uninterrupted view of every plantation which we passed. As they very much resemble each other in their general features, a description of one of them will be with a little variation applicable to all. Fortunately for me, a slight accident to our machinery, which delayed us fifteen or twenty minutes, in front of one of the finest plantations below New-Orleans, enabled me to put in practice a short system of *espionage* upon the premises, from the main top, with my spy-glass, that introduced me into the very *sanctum* of the enchanting ornamental gardens, in which the palace-like edifice was half-embowered.

The house was quadrangular, with a high steep Dutch roof, immensely large, and two stories in height; the basement or lower story being constructed of brick, with a massive colonnade of the same materials on all sides of the building. This basement was raised to a level with the summit of the levée, and formed the ground-work or basis of the edifice, which was built of wood, painted white, with Venetian blinds, and latticed verandas, supported by slender and graceful pillars, running round every side of the dwelling. Along the whole western front, festooned in massive folds, hung a dark-green curtain, which is dropped along the whole length of the balcony in a summer's afternoon, not only excluding the burning rays of the sun, but inviting the inmates to a cool and refreshing *siesta*, in some one of the half dozen network hammocks, which we discovered suspended in the veranda. The basement seemed wholly unoccupied, and probably was no more than an over-ground cellar. At each extremity of the piazza was a broad and spacious flight of steps, descending into the garden which enclosed the dwelling on every side.

Situated about two hundred yards back from the river, the approach to it was by a lofty massive gateway which entered upon a wide gravelled walk, bordered by dark foliaged orange trees, loaded with their golden fruit. Pomegranate, fig, and lemon trees, shrubs, plants and exotics of every clime and variety, were dispersed in profusion over this charming *parterre*. Double palisades of lemon and orange trees surrounded the spot, forming one of the loveliest and most elegant rural retirements, that imagination could create or romantic ambition desire. About half a mile in the rear of the dwelling, I observed a large brick building with lofty chimneys resembling towers. This was the sugar-house, wherein the cane undergoes its several transmutations, till that state of *perfection* is obtained, which renders it marketable.

On the left and diagonally from the dwelling house we noticed a very neat, pretty village, containing about forty small snow-white cottages, all precisely alike, built around a pleasant square, in the centre of which, was a grove or cluster of magnificent sycamores. Near by, suspended from a belfry, was the bell which called the slaves to and from their work and meals. This village was their residence, and under the shade of the trees in the centre of the square, we could discern troops of little ebony urchins from the age of eight years downward, all too young to work in the field, at their play—under the charge of an old, crippled *gouvernante*, who, being past "field service," was thus promoted in the "home department."

This plantation was about one mile and a half in depth from the river, terminating, like all in lower Louisiana, in an impenetrable cypress swamp; and about two miles in breadth by the levée. About one half was waving with the rich long-leafed cane, and agreeably variegated, exhibiting every delicate shade from the brightest yellow to the darkest green. A small portion of the remainder was in corn, which grows luxuriantly in this country, though but little cultivated; and the rest lay in fallow, into which a portion of every plantation is thrown, alternately, every two years.

By the time I had completed my observations, spying the richness, rather than "the nakedness" of the land, the engineer had arranged the machinery and we were again in motion; passing rapidly by rich gardens, spacious avenues, tasteful villas, and extensive fields of cane, bending to the light breeze with the wavy motion of the sea. Just before sunset we passed the site of the old fort St. Mary, and in half an hour after, swept round into the magnificent curve denominated the "English Turn."[3] As we sailed along, gay parties, probably returning from and going to, the city, on horseback, in barouches and carriages, were passing along the level road within the levée; their heads and shoulders being only visible above it, gave to the whole cavalcade a singularly ludicrous appearance—a strange bobbing of heads, hats and feathers, suggesting the idea of a new genus of locomotives amusing themselves upon the green sward.

Much to our regret, we did not arrive opposite the "battle ground" till some time after sunset. But we were in some measure remunerated for our disappointment, by gazing down upon the scene of the conflict from aloft, while as bright and clear a moon as ever shed its mellow radiance over a southern landscape, poured its full flood of light upon the now quiet battle field. I could distinguish that it was under cultivation, and that princely dwellings were near and around it; and my ear told me as we sailed swiftly by, that where shouts of conflict and carnage once broke fiercely upon the air, now floated the lively notes of cheerful music, which were wafted over the waters to the ship, falling pleasantly upon the ear.

The lights and habitations along the shore now became more frequent. Luggers, manned by negroes, light skiffs, with a solitary occupant in each, and now and then a dark hulled vessel, her lofty sails, reflecting the bright moon light, appearing like snowy clouds in the clear blue sky, were rapidly and in increasing numbers, continually gliding by us. By these certain indications we knew that we were not far from the goal so long the object of our wishes.

We had been anticipating during the morning an early arrival, when the panorama of the crescent city should burst upon our view enriched, by the mellow rays of a southern sun, with every variety of light and shade that could add to the beauty or novelty of the scene. But our sanguine anticipations were not to be realized. The shades of night had long fallen over the town, when, as we swiftly moved forward, anxiously trying to penetrate the obscurity, an interminable line of lights gradually opened in quick succession upon our view; and a low hum, like the far off roaring of the sea, with the heavy and irregular tolling of a deep mouthed bell, was borne over the waves upon the evening breeze, mingling at intervals with loud calls far away on the shore, and fainter replies still more distant. The fierce and incessant baying of dogs, and as we approached nearer, the sound of many voices, as in a tumult;—and anon, the wild, clear, startling notes of a bugle, waking the slumbering echoes on the opposite shore, succeeded by the solitary voice of some lonely singer, blended with the thrumming notes of a guitar, falling with melancholy cadence upon the ear—all gave indications that we were rapidly approaching the termination of our voyage.

In a few minutes, as we still shot onward, we could trace a thousand masts, penciled distinctly with all their network rigging upon the clear evening sky. We moved swiftly in among them; and gradually checking her speed, the tow-boat soon came nearly to a full stop, and casting off the ship astern, rounded to and left us along side of a Salem ship, which lay outside of a tier "six deep." When the bustle and confusion of making fast had subsided, we began our preparations to go on shore. So anxious were we once more to tread "terra firma," that we determined not to wait for a messenger to go half a mile for a carriage, but to walk through the gayly lighted streets to our hotel in Canal-street, more than a mile distant. So after much trouble in laying planks, for the surer footing of the ladies, from gangway to gangway, we safely reached, after crossing half a dozen ships, the firm, immoveable Levée. I will now briefly relate the little history of our truly elegant brig, as I partially promised to do in my last, and conclude this long, long letter.

Her commander was formerly an officer of the United States navy. He is a graduate of Harvard University, and presents in his person the admirable union of the polished gentleman, finished scholar, and practical seaman. Inheriting a princely fortune from a bachelor uncle, he returned to Massachusetts, his native state, and built according to his own taste the beautiful vessel he now commands. He has made in her one voyage to India, and two up the Mediterranean, and is now at this port to purchase a cargo of cotton for the European market. His officers are gentlemen of education and nautical science; his equals and companions in the cabin, though his subordinates on the deck.

If the imagination of the lonely sailor, as he mechanically paces his midnight watch, creates an Utopia in the wide ocean of futurity, if there be a limit to the enjoyment of a refined seaman's wishes, or a "ne plus ultra," to his ambition, they must all be realized and achieved, by the sole command

and control of a vessel so correctly beautiful as the D——; so ably officered and manned, so opulent with every luxury, comfort, and convenience, and free as the winds to go and come over the "dark blue sea," obedient alone to the uncontrolled will and submissive to the lightest pleasure of her absolute commander.

FOOTNOTE

[3] Tradition saith, that some British vessels of war pursuing some American vessels up the river, on arriving at this place gave up the pursuit as useless, and *turned* back to the Balize.

Another tradition saith that John Bull chasing some American ships up the river, thought, in his wisdom, when he arrived at this bend, that this was but another of the numerous outlets of the hydra-headed Mississippi, and supposing the Yankee ships were taking advantage of it to escape to the sea—he *turned* about and followed his way back; again, determined, as school boys say, to "head them!"

VIII

How delightfully comfortable one feels, and how luxuriantly disposed to quiet,—after having been tossed, and bruised, and tumbled about, *sans ceremonie,* like a bale of goods, or a printer's devil, for many long weary days and nights upon the slumberless sea—to be once more cosily established in a smiling, elegant little parlour, carpeted, curtained, and furnished with every tasteful convenience that a comfort loving, home-made bachelor could covet. In such a pleasant sitting-room am I now most enviably domesticated, and every thing around me contributes to the happiness of my situation. A cheerful coal-fire burns in the grate—(for the day is cloudy, misty, drizzly, foggy, and chilly, which is the best definition I can give you, as yet, of a wet December's day in New-Orleans,)—diffusing an agreeable temperature throughout the room, and adding, by contrast with the dark gloomy streets, seen indistinctly through the moist glass, to the enjoyment of my comforts. I am now seated by my writing-desk at a table, drawn at an agreeable distance from the fire-place—and fully convinced that a man never feels so comfortably, as when ensconced in a snug parlour on a rainy day.

A statue of dazzling ebony, by name Antoine, to which the slightest look or word will give instant animation, stands in the centre of the room, contrasting beautifully in colour with the buff paper-hangings and crimson curtains. He is a slave—about seventeen years of age, and a bright, intelligent, active boy, nevertheless—placed at my disposal as *valet* while I remain here, by the kind attention of my obliging hostess, Madame H——. He serves me in a thousand capacities, as post-boy, cicerone, &c. and is on the whole, an extremely useful and efficient attaché.

Our party having safely landed on the Levée, nearly opposite Rue Marigny, we commenced our long, yet in anticipation, delightful walk to our hotel. We had disembarked about a quarter of a league below the cathedral, from the front of which, just after we landed, the loud report of the evening gun broke over the city, rattling and reverberating through the long massively built streets, like the echoing of distant thunder along mountain ravines. On a firm, smooth, gravelled walk elevated about four feet, by a gradual ascent from the street—one side open to the river, and the other lined with the "Pride of China," or India tree, we pursued our way to Chartres-street, the "Broadway" of New-Orleans. The moon shone with uncommon brilliancy, and thousands, even in this lower faubourg, were abroad, enjoying the beauty and richness of the scene. Now, a trio of lively young Frenchmen would pass us, laughing and conversing gayly upon some merry subject, followed by a slow moving and stately figure, whose haughty tread, and dark *roquelaure* gathered with classic elegance around his form in graceful folds, yet so arranged as to conceal every feature beneath his slouched *sombrero*, except a burning, black, penetrating eye,—denoted the exiled Spaniard.

We passed on—and soon the lively sounds of the French language, uttered by soft voices, were heard nearer and nearer, and the next moment, two or three duenna-like old ladies, remarkable for their "embonpoint" dimensions, preceded a bevy of fair girls, without that most hideous of all excrescences, with which women see fit to disfigure their heads, denominated a "bonnet"—their brown, raven or auburn hair floating in ringlets behind them.

There was one—a dark-locked girl—a superb creature, over whose head and shoulders, secured above her forehead by a brilliant which in the clear moon burned like a star, waved the folds of a snow-white veil in the gentle breeze, created by her motion as she glided gracefully along. She was a Castilian; and the mellow tones of her native land gave richness to the light elegance of the French, as she breathed it like music from her lips.

As we passed on, the number of promenaders increased, but scarcely a lady was now to be seen. Every other gentleman we met was enveloped in a cloud, not of bacchanalian, but tobacconalian incense, which gave a peculiar atmosphere to the Levée.

Every, or nearly every gentleman carried a sword cane, apparently, and occasionally the bright hilt of a Spanish knife, or dirk, would gleam for an instant in the moon-beams from the open bosom of its possessor, as, with the lowering brow, and active tread of wary suspicion, he moved rapidly by us, his roundabout thrown over the left shoulder and secured by the sleeves in a knot under the arm, which was thrust into his breast, while the other arm was at liberty to attend to his segar, or engage in any mischief to which its owner might be inclined. This class of men are very numerous here. They are easily distinguished by their shabby appearance, language, and foreign way of wearing their apparel. In groups—promenading, lounging, and sleeping upon the seats along the Levée—we passed several hundred of this *canaille* of Orleans, before we arrived at the "Parade," the public square in front of the cathedral. They are mostly Spaniards and Portuguese, though there are among them representatives from all the unlucky families which, at the building of Babel, were dispersed over the earth. As to their mode and means of existence, I have not as yet informed myself; but I venture to presume that they resort to no means beneath the dignity of "caballeros!"

After passing the market on our right, a massive colonnade, about two hundred and fifty feet in length, we left the Levée, and its endless tier of shipping which had bordered one side of our walk all the way, and passing under the China-trees, that still preserved their unbroken line along the river, we crossed Levée-street, a broad, spacious esplanade, running along the front of the main body or block of the city, separating it from the Levée, and forming a magnificent thoroughfare along the whole extensive river-line. From this high-way streets shoot off at right angles, till they terminate in the swamp somewhat less than a league back from the river. I have termed New-Orleans the crescent city in one of my letters, from its being built around the segment of a circle formed by a graceful curve of the river at this place. Though the water, or shore-line, is very nearly semi-circular, the Levée-street, above mentioned, does not closely follow the shore, but is broken into two angles, from which the streets diverge as before mentioned. These streets are again intersected by others running parallel with the Levée-street, dividing the city into squares, except where the perpendicular streets meet the angles, where necessarily the "squares" are lessened in breadth at the extremity nearest the river, and occasionally form pentagons and parallelograms, with *oblique* sides, if I may so express it.

After crossing Levée-street, we entered Rue St. Pierre, which issues from it south of the grand square. This square is an open green, surrounded by a lofty iron railing, within which troops of boys, whose sports carried my thoughts away to "home, sweet home," were playing, shouting and merry making, precisely as we used to do in days long past, when the harvest-moon would invite us from our dwellings to the village green, where many and many a joyful night we have played till the magic voice of our good old Scotch preceptor was heard from the door of his little cottage under the elms, "Laads, laads, it's unco time ye were in bed, laads," warning us to our sleepy pillows. The front of this extensive square was open to the river, bordered with its dark line of ships; on each side were blocks of rusty looking brick buildings of Spanish and French construction, with projecting balconies, heavy cornices, and lofty jalousies or barricaded windows. The lower stories of these buildings were occupied by retailers of fancy wares, vintners, segar manufacturers, dried fruit sellers, and all the other members of the innumerable occupations, to which the volatile, ever ready Frenchman can always turn himself and a *sous* into the bargain. As we passed along, these shops were all lighted up, and the happy faces, merry songs, and gay dances therein, occasionally contrasted with the shrill tone of feminine anger in a foreign tongue, and the loud, fierce, rapid voices of men mingling in dispute, added to the novelty and amusement of our walk. I enumerated ten, out of seventeen successive shops or *cabarets*, upon the shelves of which I could discover nothing but myriads of claret and Madeira bottles, tier upon tier to the ceiling; and from this fact I came to the conclusion, that some of the worthy citizens of New-Orleans must be most unconscionable "wine-bibbers," if not "publicans and sinners," as subsequent observation has led me to surmise.

On the remaining side of this square stood the cathedral, its dark moorish-looking towers flinging their vast shadows far over the water. The whole front of the large edifice was thrown into deep shade, so that when we approached, it presented one black mingled mass, frowning in stern and majestic silence upon the surrounding scene.

Leaving this venerable building at the right, we turned into Chartres-street, the second parallel with the Levée, and the most fashionable, as well as greatest business street in the city. As we proceeded, *cafés*, confectioners, fancy stores, millineries, parfumeurs, &c. &c., were passed in rapid succession; each one of them presenting something new, and always something to strike the attention of strangers, like ourselves, for the first time in the only "foreign" city in the United States.

At the corner of one of the streets intersecting Chartres-street—Rue St. Louis I believe—we passed a large building, the lofty basement story of which was lighted with a glare brighter than that of noon. In the back ground, over the heads of two or three hundred loud-talking, noisy gentlemen, who were promenading and vehemently gesticulating, in all directions, through the spacious room—I discovered a bar, with its peculiar dazzling array of glasses and decanters containing "spirits"—not of "the vasty deep" certainly, but of whose potent spells many were apparently trying the power, by frequent libations. This building—of which and its uses more anon—I was informed, was the "French" or "New Exchange." After passing Rue Toulouse, the streets began to assume a new character; the buildings were loftier and more modern—the signs over the doors bore English names, and the characteristic arrangements of a northern dry goods store were perceived, as we peered in at the now closing doors of many stores by which we passed. We had now attained the upper part of Chartres-street, which is occupied almost exclusively by retail and wholesale dry goods dealers, jewellers, booksellers, &c., from the northern states, and I could almost realize that I was taking an evening promenade in Cornhill, so great was the resemblance.

As we successively crossed Rues Conti, Bienville and Douane, and looked down these long straight avenues, the endless row of lamps, suspended in the middle of these streets, as well as in all others in New-Orleans, by chains or ropes, extended from house to house across, had a fine and brilliant effect, which we delayed for a moment on the flag-stone to admire, endeavouring to reach with our eyes the almost invisible extremity of this line of flame. Just before we reached the head of Chartres-street, near Bienville, in the immediate vicinity of which is the boarding house of Madame H— —, where we intended to take rooms, our way was impeded by a party of gentlemen in violent altercation in English and French, who completely blocked up the "trottoir." "Sir," said one of the party—a handsome, resolute-looking young man—in a calm deliberate voice, which was heard above every other, and listened to as well—"Sir, you have grossly insulted me, and I shall expect from you, immediately—before we separate—an acknowledgment, adequate to the injury." "Monsieur," replied a young Frenchman whom he had addressed, in French, "Monsieur, I never did insult you—a gentleman never insults! you have misunderstood me, and refuse to listen to a candid explanation." "The explanation you have given sir," reiterated the first speaker, "is not sufficient—it is a subterfuge;" here many voices mingled in loud confusion, and a renewed and more violent altercation ensued which prevented our hearing distinctly; and as we had already crossed to the opposite side of the street, having ladies under escort, we rapidly passed on our way, but had not gained half a square before the clamour increased to an uproar—steel struck steel—one, then another pistol was discharged in rapid succession—"guards!" "gens d'armes, *gens d'armes*," "guards! guards!" resounded along the streets, and we arrived at our hotel, just in time to escape being run down, or run through at their option probably, by half a dozen gens d'armes in plain blue uniforms, who were rushing with drawn swords in their hands to the scene of contest, perfectly well assured in our own minds, that we had most certainly arrived at New-Orleans!

Though affairs of the kind just described are no uncommon thing here, and are seldom noticed in the papers of the day—yet the following allusion to the event of last evening may not be uninteresting to you, and I will therefore copy it, and terminate my letter with the extract.

"An affray occurred last night in the vicinity of Bienville-street, in which one young gentleman was severely wounded by the discharge of a pistol, and another slightly injured by a dirk. An "*affaire d'honneur*" originated from this, and the parties met this morning. Dr. — — of New-York, one of the principals, was mortally wounded by his antagonist M. Le— — of this city."

IX

I know of no sensation so truly delightful and exciting as that experienced by a traveller, when he makes his *debut* in a strange and interesting city. These feelings have attended me before, in many other and more beautiful places; but when I sallied out the morning after my arrival, to survey this "Key of the Great Valley," I enjoyed them again with almost as much zest, as when, a novice to cities and castellated piles, I first gazed in silent wonder upon the immense dome which crowns Beacon Hill, and lingered to survey with a fascinated eye the princely edifices that surround it.

I shall ever remember, with the liveliest emotions, my first visit to Boston—the first "city," (what a charm to a country lad in the appellation) I had ever seen. It was a delightful summer's morning, when, urged forward by a gentle wind, our little, green-painted, coasting packet entered the magnificent harbour, which, broken and diversified with its beautiful islands, lay outspread before us like a chain of lakes sleeping among hills. With what romantic and youthful associations did I then gaze upon the lonely sea-washed monument, as we sailed rapidly by it, where the famous pirate, "Nick," murdered his mate; and a little farther on, upon a pleasant green island, where the bloody "Robert Kidd" buried treasures that no man could number, or find!—With what patriotism, almost kindled into a religion, did I gaze upon the noble heights of Dorchester as they lifted their twin summits to the skies on our left, and upon the proud eminence far to the right, where Warren expired and liberty was born!

I well remember with what wild enthusiasm I bounded on shore ere the vessel had quite reached it, and with juvenile elasticity, ran, rather than walked, up through the hurry and bustle that always attend Long Wharf. With what veneration I looked upon the spot, in State-street, where the first American blood was shed by British soldiers! With what reverence I paced "Old Cornhill"—and with what deep respect I gazed upon the venerable "Old South," the scene of many a revolutionary incident! The site of the "Liberty Tree"—the "King's" Chapel, where Lionel Lincoln was married—

the wharf, from which the tea was poured into the dock by the disguised citizens, and a hundred other scenes and places of interesting associations were visited, and gave me a pleasure that I fear can never so perfectly be felt again. For then, my feelings were young, fresh and buoyant, and my curiosity, as in after life, had never been glutted and satiated by the varieties and novelties of our variegated world. Even the "cannon-ball" embedded in the tower of Brattle-street church, was an object of curiosity; the building in which Franklin worked when an apprentice, was not passed by, unvisited; and the ancient residence of "Job Pray" was gazed upon with a kind of superstitious reverence. I do not pretend to compare my present feelings with those of that happy period. Although my curiosity may not be so eager as then, it is full as persevering; and though I may not experience the same lively gratification, in viewing strange and novel scenes, that I felt in boyhood, I certainly do as much rational and intellectual pleasure; and obtain more valuable and correct information than I could possibly gain, were I still guided by the more volatile curiosity of youth.

In spite of our fatigue of the preceding evening, and the luxury of a soft, firm bed, wherein one could sleep without danger of being capsized by a lee-lurch—a blessing we had not enjoyed for many a long and weary night—we were up with the sun and prepared for a stroll about the city. Our first place of destination was the market-house, a place which in almost every commercial city is always worthy the early notice of a stranger, as it is a kind of "House of Representatives" of the city to which it belongs, where, during the morning, delegates from almost every family are found studying the interests of their constituents by judicious negotiations for comestibles. If the market at New-Orleans represents that city, so truly does New-Orleans represent every other city and nation upon earth. I know of none where is congregated so great a variety of the human species, of every language and colour. Not only natives of the well known European and Asiatic countries are here to be met with, but occasionally Persians, Turks, Lascars, Maltese, Indian sailors from South America and the Islands of the sea, Hottentots, Laplanders, and, for aught I know to the contrary, Symmezonians.

Now should any philanthropic individual, anxious for the advancement of the noble science of physiognomy, wish to survey the motley countenances of these goodly personages, let him on some bright and sunny morning bend his steps toward the market-house; for there, in all their variety and shades of colouring they may be seen, and *heard*. If a painting could affect the sense of hearing as well as that of sight, this market multitude would afford the artist an inimitable original for the representation upon his canvass of the "confusion of tongues."

As we sallied from our hotel to commence our first tour of sight seeing, the vast city was just waking into life. Our sleepy servants were opening the shutters, and up and down the street a hundred of their drowsy brethren were at the same enlightening occupation. Black women, with huge baskets of rusks, rolls and other appurtenances of the breakfast table, were crying, in loud shrill French, their "stock in trade," followed by milk-criers, and butter-criers and criers of every thing but tears: for they all seemed as merry as the morning, saluting each other gayly as they met, "Bo' shoo Mumdsal"—"Moshoo! adieu," &c. &c., and shooting their rude shafts of African wit at each other with much vivacity and humor.

We turned down Canal-street—the broadest in New-Orleans, and destined to be the most magnificent. Its breadth I do not know, correctly, but it is certainly one half wider than Broadway opposite the Park.—Through its centre runs a double row of young trees, which, when they arrive at maturity, will form the finest mall in the United States, unless the *esplanade*—a beautiful mall at the south part of the city, should excel it.

From the head of Canal-street we entered Levée-street, leaving the custom house, a large, plain, yellow stuccoed building upon our right, near which is a huge, dark coloured, unshapely pile of brick, originally erected for a *Bethel church* for seamen, but never finished, and seldom occupied, except by itinerant showmen, with their wonders. Levée-street had already begun to assume a bustling, commerce-like appearance. The horse-drays were trundling rapidly by, sometimes four abreast, racing to different parts of the Levée for their loads—and upon each was mounted a ragged negro, who, as Jehu-like he drove along, standing upright and unsupported, resembled "Phaeton in the suds"—rather than "Phaeton the god-like."

The stores on our left were all open, and nearly every one of them, for the first two squares, was occupied as a clothing or hat store, and kept by Americans; that is to say, Anglo Americans as distinguished from the Louisianian French, who very properly, and proudly too, assume the national appellation, which we of the English tongue have so haughtily arrogated to ourselves. As we approached the market, French stores began to predominate, till one could readily imagine himself, aided by the sound of the French language, French faces and French goods on all sides, to be traversing a street in Havre or Marseilles. Though I do not pretend to be a critical connoisseur in French, yet I could discover a marked and striking difference between the language I heard spoken every where and by all classes, in the streets, and the Parisian, or trans-Atlantic French. The principal difference seems to be in their method of contracting or clipping their words, and consequently varying, more or less, the pronunciation of every termination susceptible of change. The vowels *o* and *e* are more open, and the *a* is flatter than in the genuine French, and often loses altogether its emphatic fulness; while *u*, corrupted from its difficult, but peculiarly soft sound, is almost universally pronounced as full and plain as *oo* in moon. This difference is of course only in pronunciation; the same literature, and consequently the same words and orthography, being common both to the creole and European. The sun had already risen, when I arrived, after a delightful walk, at the "marché."—This is a fine building consisting of a long, lofty roof, supported by rows of columns on every side. It is constructed of brick, and stuccoed; and, either by intention or an effect of the humid atmosphere of this climate, is of a dingy cream colour.

A broad passage runs through the whole length of the structure, each side of which is lined with stalls, where some one, of no particular colour, presides; and before every pillar, the shining face of a blackee may be seen glistening from among his vegetables. As I moved on through a dense mass of negroes, mulattoes, and non-descripts of every shade, from "sunny hue to sooty," all balancing their baskets skilfully upon their heads, my ears were assailed with sounds stranger and more complicated than I ever imagined could be rung upon that marvellous instrument the human tongue. The "langue des halles"—the true "Billingsgate" was not only here perfected but improved upon; the gods and goddesses of the London mart might even take lessons from these daughters of Afric, who, enthroned upon a keg, or three-legged stool, each morning hold their *levée*, and dispense their esculent blessings to the famishing citizens. During the half hour I remained in the market, I did not see one white person to fifty blacks. It appears that here servants do all the marketing, and that gentlemen and ladies do not, as in Boston, Philadelphia, and elsewhere, visit the market-places themselves, and select their own provision for their tables. The market-place in Philadelphia is quite a general resort and promenade for early-rising gentlemen, and it is certainly well worth one's while to visit it more than once, not only for the gratification of the palate and the eye, by the inviting display of epicurean delicacies, but to become more particularly acquainted with the general habits and manners of the country people, who always constitute the greater portion of the multitude at a market. Among them are individuals from every little hamlet and village for ten or fifteen miles around the city, and by studying these people, a tolerably good idea may be formed by a stranger of the manners and customs of the inhabitants, (that is, the farming class) of the vicinity.

But here, there is no temptation of the kind to induce one to visit the market in the city more than once. He will see nothing to gratify the spirit of inquiry or observation, in the ignorant, careless-hearted slaves, whose character presents neither variety nor interest. However well they may represent their brethren in the city and on the neighbouring sugar plantations, they cannot be ranked among the class of their fellow-beings denominated citizens, and consequently, are not to be estimated by a stranger in judging of this community.

So far as regards the intrinsic importance of this market, it is undoubtedly equal to any other in America. Vegetables and fruits of all climates are displayed in bountiful profusion in the vegetable stalls, while the beef and fish-market is abundantly supplied, though necessarily without that endless variety to be found in Atlantic cities.

In front, upon the water, were double lines of market and fish-boats, secured to the Levée, forming a small connecting link of the long chain of shipping and steamboats that extend for a league in front of the city. At the lower part of the town lie generally those ships, which having their cargoes on board, have dropped down the river to await their turn to be towed to sea. Fronting this station are no stores, but several elegant private dwellings, constructed after the combined French and Spanish style of architecture, almost embowered in dark, evergreen foliage, and surrounded by parterres. The next station above, and immediately adjoining this, is usually occupied by vessels, which, just arrived, have not yet obtained a berth where they can discharge their cargoes; though not unfrequently ships here discharge and receive their freight, stretching along some distance up the Levée to the link of market-boats just mentioned.

From the market to the vicinity of Bienville-street, lies an extensive tier of shipping, often "six deep," discharging and receiving cargo, or waiting for freight. The next link of the huge chain is usually occupied by Spanish and French coasting vessels,—traders to Mexico, Texas, Florida, &c. These are usually polaccas, schooners, and other small craft—and particularly black, rakish craft, some of them are in appearance. It would require but little exercise of the imagination, while surveying these truculent looking clippers, to fancy any one of them, clothed in canvass and bounding away upon the broad sea, the "*Black flag*" flying aloft, the now gunless deck bristling with five eighteens to a side; and her indolent, smoking, dark faced crew exchanging their jack-knives for sabres and pistols. There was an instance of recent occurrence, where a ship was boarded and plundered by a well-armed and strongly manned schooner, in company with which, under the peaceful guise of a merchantman she had been towed down the river six days previous.

Next to this station (for as you will perceive, the whole Levée is divided into *stations* appropriated to peculiar classes of shipping,) commences the range of steamboats, or steamers, as they are usually termed here, rivaling in magnitude the extensive line of ships below. The appearance of so large a collection of steamboats is truly novel, and must always strike a stranger with peculiar interest.

The next station, though it presents a more humble appearance than the others, is not the least interesting. Here are congregated the primitive navies of Indiana, Ohio, and the adjoining states, manned (I have not understood whether they are *officered* or not) by "real Kentucks"—"Buck eyes"—"Hooshers"—and "Snorters." There were about two hundred of these craft without masts, consisting of "flat-boats," (which resemble, only being much shorter, the "Down East" gundalow, (gondola) so common on the rivers of Maine,) and "keel-boats," which are one remove from the flat-boat, having some pretensions to a keel; they somewhat resemble freighting canal-boats. Besides these are "arks," most appropriately named, their *contents* having probably some influence with their god-fathers in selecting an appellation, and other non-descript-craft. These are filled with produce of all kinds, brought from the "Upper country," (as the north western states are termed here) by the very farmers themselves who have raised it;—also, horses, cattle, hogs, poultry, mules, and every other thing raiseable and saleable are piled into these huge flats, which an old farmer and half a dozen Goliaths of sons can begin and complete in less than a week, from the felling of the first tree to the driving of the last pin.

When one of these arks is completed, and "every beast that is good for food" by sevens and scores, male and female, and every fowl of the air by sevens and fifties, are entered into the ark,—then entereth in the old man with his family by "males" only, and the boat is committed to the current, and after the space of many days arriveth and resteth at this Ararat of all "Up country" Noahs.

These boats, on arriving here, are taken to pieces and sold as lumber, while their former owners with well-lined purses return home as deck passengers on board steamboats. An immense quantity of whiskey from

Pittsburg and Cincinnati, besides, is brought down in these boats, and not unfrequently, they are crowded with slaves for the southern market.

The late excellent laws relative to the introduction of slaves, however, have checked, in a great measure, this traffic here, and the Mississippi market at Natchez has consequently become inundated, by having poured into it, in addition to its usual stock, the Louisianian supply. I understand that the legislature of this rich and enterprising state is about to pass a law similar to the one above mentioned, which certainly will be incalculably to her advantage.

The line of flats may be considered the last link of the great chain of shipping in front of New-Orleans, unless we consider as attached to it a kind of dock adjoining, where ships and steamers often lie, either worn out or undergoing repairs. From this place to the first station I have mentioned, runs along the Levée, fronting the shipping, an uninterrupted block of stores, (except where they are intersected by streets,) some of which are lofty and elegant, while others are clumsy piles of French and Spanish construction, browned and blackened by age.

X

The last three days I have spent in perambulating the city, hearing, seeing, and visiting every thing worthy the notice of a Yankee, (and consequently an inquisitive) tourist.

As I shall again have occasion to introduce you among the strange and motley groups, and interesting scenes of the Levée, I will not now resume the thread of my narrative, broken by the conclusion of my last letter, but take you at once into the "terra incognita" of this city of contrarieties.

The evening of my visit to the market, through the politeness of Monsieur D., a young Frenchman who distinguished himself in the great "Three Days" at Paris, and to whom I had a letter of introduction, was passed amid the gayety and brilliancy of a French assembly-room. The building in which this ball was held, is adjacent to the Theatre d'Orleans, and devoted, I believe, exclusively to public parties, which are held here during the winter months, or more properly, "the season," almost every night. The occasion on which I attended, was one of peculiar interest. It was termed the "Children's ball;" and it is given at regular intervals throughout the gay months. I have not learned the precise object of this ball, or how it is conducted; but these are unimportant. I merely wish to introduce to you the dazzling crowd gathered there, so that you may form some conception of the manner and appearance of the lively citizens of this lively city, who seem disposed to remunerate themselves for the funereal and appalling silence of the long and gloomy season, when "pestilence walketh abroad at noon-day," by giving way to the full current of life and spirits. Adopting, literally, "Dum vivimus vivamus," for their motto and their "rule of faith and practice," they manage during the winter not only to make up for the privations of summer, but to execute about as much dancing, music, laughing, and dissipation, as would serve any reasonably disposed, staid, and sober citizens, for three or four years, giving them withal from January to January for the perpetration thereof.

After taking a light supper at *home*, as I already call my hotel, which consisted of claret, macaroni, cranberries, peaches, little plates of fresh grapes, several kinds of cakes and other bonbons, spread out upon a long polished mahogany table, resembling altogether more the display upon a confectioner's counter than the *table d'hote* of a hotel, in company with Monsieur D. I prepared to walk to the scene of the evening's amusement. But on gaining the street we observed the "omnibus" still at its stand at the intersection of Canal and Chartres streets. The driver, already upon his elevated station, with his bugle at his lips, was sounding his "signal to make sail," as we should say of a ship; and thereupon, being suddenly impressed with the advantages the sixteen legs of his team had over our four, in accomplishing the mile before us, we without farther reflection, sprang forthwith into the invitingly open door at the end of the vehicle, and the next instant found ourselves comfortably seated, with about a dozen others, "in omnibus."

There are two of these carriages which run from Canal-street through the whole length of Chartres-street, by the public square, and along the noble esplanade between the Levée and the main body of the city, as far as the rail-road; the whole distance being about two miles. The two vehicles start simultaneously from either place, every half-hour, and consequently change stands with each other alternately throughout the day. They commence running early in the morning, and are always on the move and crowded with passengers till sun-down. For a "bit" (twelve-and-a-half cents) as it is denominated here, one can ride the whole distance, or if he choose, but a hundred yards—it is all the same to the knight of the whip, who mounted on the box in front, guides his "four-in-hand" with the skill of a professor.

As we drove through the long, narrow and dusky street, the wholesale mercantile houses were "being" closed, while the retail stores and fancy shops, were "being" brilliantly lighted up. Carriages, horsemen, and noisy drays, with their noisier draymen, were rapidly moving in all directions, while every individual upon the "trottoirs" was hurrying, as though some important business of the day had been forgotten, or not yet completed. All around presented the peculiar noise and bustle which always prevail throughout the streets of a commercial city at the close of the day.

Leaving our omniferous vehicle with its omnifarious cargo—among whom, fore and aft, the chattering of half a dozen languages had all at once, as we rode along, unceasingly assailed our ears—at the head of Rue St. Pierre, we proceeded toward Orleans-street. Directly on quitting the omnibus we passed the famous Calaboos, or Calabozo, the city prison, so celebrated by all seamen who have made the voyage to New-Orleans, and who, in their "long yarns" upon the forecastle, in their weary watches, fail not to clothe it with every horror of which the Calcutta black hole, or the Dartmoor prison—two horrible bugbears to sailors—could boast. Its external appearance, however, did not strike me as very appealing. It is a long, plain, plastered, blackened building, with grated windows, looking gloomy enough, but not more so than a common country jail. It is built close upon the street, and had not my companion observed as we passed along, "That is the Calaboos," I should not probably have remarked it. On the corner above, and fronting the "square," is the guard-house, or quarters of the gens d'armes. Several of them in their plain blue uniforms and side arms, were lounging about the corner as we passed, mingling and conversing with persons in citizens' dress. A glance *en passant* through an open door, disclosed an apparently well-filled armory. A few minutes walk through an obscure and miserably lighted part of Rues St. Pierre and Royale, brought us into Orleans-street, immediately in the vicinity of its theatre. This street for some distance on either side of the assembly-room, was lighted with the brightness of noon-day; not, indeed, by the solitary lamps which, "few and far between," were suspended across the streets, but by the glare of reflectors and chandeliers from coffee-houses, restaurateurs, confectionaries and fancy stores, which were clustered around that nucleus of pleasure, the French theatre.

We were in the French part of the city; but there was no apparent indication that we were not really in France. Not an American ("Anglo") building was to be seen, in the vicinity, nor scarcely an American face or voice discoverable among the numerous, loud-talking, chattering crowd of every grade and colour, congregated before the doors of the ball-room and cafés adjoining. Before ascending to the magnificent hall where the gay dancers were assembled, we repaired to an adjoining café, *à la mode* New-Orleans, with a pair of Monsieur D.'s friends—whom we encountered in the lobby while negotiating for tickets—to overhaul the evening papers, and if need there should be, recruit our spirits. A French coffee-house is a place well worth visiting by a stranger, more especially a Yankee stranger. I will therefore detain you a little longer from the brilliant congregation of beauty and gallantry in the assembly room, and introduce you for a moment into this café and to its inmates. As the coffee houses here do not differ materially from each other except in size and richness of decoration, though some of them certainly are more fashionable resorts than others, the description of one of them will enable you perhaps to form some idea of other similar establishments in this city. Though their usual denomination is "coffee-house," they have no earthly, whatever may be their spiritual, right to such a distinction; it is merely a "*nomme de profession*," assumed, I know not for what object. We entered from the street, after passing round a large Venetian screen within the door, into a spacious room, lighted by numerous lamps, at the extremity of which stood an extensive bar, arranged, in addition to the usual array of glass ware, with innumerable French decorations. There were several attendants, some of whom spoke English, as one of the requirements of their station. This is the case of all *employés* throughout New-Orleans; nearly every store and place of public resort being provided with individuals in attendance who speak both languages. Around the room were suspended splendid engravings and fine paintings, most of them of the most licentious description, and though many of their subjects were classical, of a voluptuous and luxurious character. This is French taste however. There are suspended in the Exchange in Chartres-street—one of the most magnificent and public rooms in the city—paintings which, did they occupy an equally conspicuous situation in Merchant's Hall, in Boston, would be instantly defaced by the populace.

Around the room, beneath the paintings, were arranged many small tables, at most of which three or four individuals were seated, some alternately sipping negus and puffing their segars, which are as indispensable necessaries to a Creole at all times, as his right hand, eye-brows, and left shoulder in conversation. Others were reading newspapers, and occasionally assisting their comprehension of abstruse paragraphs, by hot "coffee," alias warm punch and slings, with which, on little japanned salvers, the active attendants were flying in all directions through the spacious room, at the beck and call of customers. The large circular bar was surrounded by a score of noisy applicants for the liquid treasures which held out to them such strong temptations. Trios, couples and units of gentlemen were promenading the well sanded floor, talking in loud tones, and gesticulating with the peculiar vehemence and rapidity of Frenchmen. Others, and by far the majority, were gathered by twos and by fours around the little tables, deeply engaged in playing that most intricate, scientific, and mathematical of games termed "Domino." This is the most common game resorted to by the Creoles. In every café and cabaret, from early in the morning, when the luxurious mint-julep has thawed out their intellects and expanded their organ of combativeness, till late at night, devotees to this childish amusement will be found clustered around the tables, with a tonic, often renewed and properly sangareed, at their elbows. Enveloped in dense clouds of tobacco-smoke issuing from their eternal segars—those inspirers of pleasant thoughts,—to whose density, with commendable perseverance and apparent good will, all in the café contribute,—they manœuvre their little dotted, black and white parallelograms with wonderful pertinacity and skill. The whole scene forcibly reminds one, if perchance their fame hath reached him, of a brace of couplets from a celebrated poem (a choral ode I believe) composed upon the ship-wreck of its author. The lines are strikingly applicable to the present subject by merely substituting "café" for "cabin," and negus-drinkers for "hogsheads and barrels."

"The café filled with thickest smoke,
Threat'ning every soul to choke:
Negus-drinkers crowding in,
Make a most infernal din."

There are certainly one hundred coffee-houses in this city—how many more, I know not,—and they have, throughout the day, a constant ingress and egress of thirsty, time-killing, news-seeking visiters. As custom authorises this frequenting of these popular places of resort, the citizens of New-Orleans do not, like those of Boston, attach any disapprobation to the houses or their visiters. And as there is, in New-Orleans, from the renewal of one half of its inhabitants every few years, and the constant influx of strangers, strictly speaking no exclusive *clique* or aristocracy, to give a tone to society and establish a standard of propriety and respectability, as among the worthy Bostonians, one cannot say to another, "It is not genteel to resort here—it will injure your reputation to be seen entering this or that café." The inhabitants have no fixed criterion of what is and what is not "respectable," in the northern acceptation of the term. They are neither guided nor restrained from following their own inclinations, by any laws of long established society, regulating their movements, and saying "thus far shalt thou go, and no farther." Consequently, every man minds his own affairs, pursues his own business or amusement, and lets his neighbours and fellow-citizens do the same; without the fear of the moral lash (not law) before his eyes, or expulsion from "caste" for doing that "in which his soul delighteth."

Thus you see that society here is a perfect democracy, presenting variety and novelty enough to a stranger, who chooses to mingle in it freely, and feels a disposition impartially to study character. But a truce to this subject for the present, as I wish to introduce you into the presence of the fair democrats, whose fame for beauty is so well established.

Forcing our way through the press around the door, we entered the lobby, from which a broad flight of steps conducted us to a first, and then a second platform, through piles of black servants in attendance upon their masters and mistresses in the ball-room. At the second landing our tickets were received, and we toiled on with difficulty toward the hall door, with our hats (which the regulations forbid our wearing even in the entrance) elevated in the air, for if placed under the arm they would have been flattened in the squeeze to the very respectable similitude of a platter, as one unlucky gentleman near me had an opportunity of testing, to his full conviction. We were soon drawn within the current setting into the ball-room, and were borne onward by the human stream over which a score or two of chapeaux waved aloft like signals of distress.—But I have already spun out my letter to a sufficient length, and lest you should cry "hold, Macduff," I will defer your introduction to the *beau monde* of New-Orleans till my next.

XI

I have endeavoured to give you, in my hastily written letters, some notion of this city—its streets, buildings, inhabitants and various novelties, as they first struck my eye; and I apprehend that I have expanded my descriptions, by minuteness of detail, to a greater length than was necessary or desirable. But the scenes, individuals, and circumstances I meet with in my erranting expeditions through the city, are such as would attract, from their novelty, the attention of a traveller from the North, and, consequently, a description of them is neither unworthy a place in his letters, nor too inconsiderable to detain the attention of an inquisitive northern reader, vegetating "at home."

On entering, from the dimly lighted lobby, the spacious and brilliant hall, illuminated with glittering chandeliers, where the beauty, and fashion, and gallantry of this merry city were assembled, I was struck with the spirit, life, and splendour of the scene. From alcoves on every side of the vast hall, raised a few steps from the floor, and separated from the area for dancing by an estrade of slender columns which formed a broad promenade quite around the room, bright eyes were glancing over the lively scene, rivalling in brilliancy the glittering gems that sparkled on brow and bosom.

There were at least five hundred persons in the hall, two-thirds of whom were spectators. On double rows of settees arranged around the room, and bordering the area, were about one hundred ladies, exclusive of half as many, seated in the alcoves. In addition to an almost impenetrable body of gentlemen standing in the vicinity of the grand entrance, the promenade above alluded to was filled with them, as they lounged along, gazing and remarking upon the beautiful faces of the dark-eyed Creoles,[4] as their expressive and lovely features were lighted up and instinct with the animation of the moment; while others, more enviable, were clustered around the alcoves—most of which were literally and truly "bowers of beauty,"—gayly conversing with their fair occupants, as they gracefully leaned over the balustrade. There were several cotillions upon the floor, and the dancers were young masters and misses—I beg their pardon—young gentlemen and ladies, from four years old and upward—who were bounding away to the lively music, as completely happy as innocence and enjoyment could make them. I never beheld a more pleasing sight. The carriage of the infantile gentlemen was graceful and easy: and they wound through the mazes of the dance with an air of manliness and elegance truly French. But the tiny demoiselles moved with the lightness and grace of fairies. Their diminutive feet, as they glided through the figure, scarcely touched the floor, and as they sprang flying away to the livelier measures of the band, they were scarcely visible, fluttering indistinctly like humming birds' wings. They were dressed with great taste in white frocks, but their hair was so arranged as completely to disfigure their heads. Some of them, not more than eight years of age, had it dressed in the extreme Parisian fashion; and the little martyrs' natural deficiency of long hair was amply remedied by that sovereign mender of the defects of nature, Monsieur le friseur. The young gentlemen were dressed also in the French mode; that is, in elaborately embroidered coatees, and richly wrought frills. Their hair, however, was suffered to grow long, and fall in graceful waves or ringlets (French children always have beautiful hair) upon their shoulders; very much as boys are represented in old fashioned prints. This is certainly more becoming than the uncouth round-head custom now prevalent in the United States, of clipping the hair short, as though boys, like sheep, needed a periodical sheering; and it cannot be denied that they both—sheep and boys—are *equally* improved in appearance by the operation.

Turning from the bright and happy faces of the children, we met on every side the delighted looks of their parents and guardians, or elder brothers and sisters, who formed a large portion of the spectators.

As I promenaded arm in arm with Monsieur D. through the room, I noticed that at one end of the hall many of the young misses (or their guardians) were so unpardonably unfashionable as to suffer their hair to float free in wild luxuriance over their necks, waving and undulating at every motion like clouds; and many of the cheerful joyous faces I gazed upon, forcibly reminded me of those which are to be met with, trudging to and from school, every day at home.

"These are the American children," observed my companion; "one half of the hall is appropriated to them, the other to the French." "What!" I exclaimed, "is there such a spirit of rivalry, jealousy, or prejudice, existing between the French and American residents here, that they cannot meet even in a ball-room without resorting to so singular a method of expressing their uncongeniality of feeling, as that of separating themselves from each other by a line of demarcation?"

"By no means," he replied; "far from it. There is, I believe, a universal unanimity of feeling among the parties. There is now no other distinction, whatever may have existed in former days, either known or admitted, than the irremediable one of language. This distinction necessarily exists, and I am of opinion ever will exist in this city in a greater or less degree. It is this which occasions the separation you behold; for, from their ignorance of each other's language,—an ignorance too prevalent here, and both inexcusable and remarkable, when we consider the advantages mutually enjoyed for their acquisition,—were they indiscriminately mingled, the result would be a confusion like that of Babel, or a constrained stiffness and reserve, the natural consequence of mutual inability to converse,—instead of that regularity and cheerful harmony which now reign throughout the crowded hall."

During our promenade through the room I had an opportunity of taking my first survey of the gay world of this city, and of viewing at my leisure the dark-eyed fascinating Creoles, whose peculiar cast of beauty and superb figures are everywhere celebrated. Of the large assembly of ladies present,—and there were nearly two hundred, "maid, wife, and widow,"—there were many very pretty, if coal-black hair, regular features, pale, clear complexions, intelligent faces, lighted up by

"Eyes that flash and burn
Beneath dark arched brows,"

and graceful figures, all of which are characteristic of the Creole, come under this definition. There were others who would be called "handsome" anywhere, except in the Green Mountains, where a pretty face and a red apple, a homely face and a lily, are pretty much synonymous terms. A few were eminently beautiful; but there was one figure, which, as my eye wandered over the brilliant assembly, fixed it in a moment. I soon learned that she was the most celebrated belle of New-Orleans.

I have certainly beheld far more beauty among the same number of ladies in a northern ball-room, than I discovered here. Almost every young lady in New-England appears pretty, with her rosy cheeks, intelligent face, and social manners. The style of beauty at the south is of a more passive kind, and excitement is requisite to make it speak to the eye; but when the possessor is animated, then the whole face, which but a few moments before was passionless and quiet, becomes radiant and illuminated with fire and intelligence; and the indolent repose of the features becomes broken by fascinating smiles, and brilliant flashes from fine dark eyes. Till this change is produced, the face of the southern lady appears plain and unattractive; and the promenader through a New-Orleans assembly-room, where there was no excitement, if such could be the case, would pronounce the majority of the ladies decidedly wanting in beauty; but let him approach and enter into conversation with one of them, and he would be delighted and surprised at the magical transformation,

"From grave to gay, from apathy to fire."

It is certain, that beauty of features and form is more general in New-England; though in grace and expression, the south has the superiority.

The difference is usually attributed to climate; but this never has been demonstrated, and the cause is still inexplicable. You are probably aware that the human form, more particularly the female, is here matured three or four years sooner than at the north. At the age of thirteen or fourteen, before their minds are properly developed, their habits formed, or their passions modified, the features of young girls become regular, their complexions delicate, and their figures attain that *tournure* and womanly grace, though "beautifully less" in their persons, found only in northern ladies, at the age of seventeen or eighteen. The beauty of the latter, though longer in coming to maturity, and less perfect, is more permanent and interesting than the infantile and bewitching loveliness of the former. In consequence of this early approach to womanhood, the duration of their personal loveliness is of proportional limitation. Being young ladies at an age that would entitle them to the appellation of children in colder climates, they must naturally retire much sooner than these from the ranks of beauty. So when northern ladies are reigning in the full pride and loveliness of their sex—every feature expanding into grace and expression—southern ladies, of equal age, are changing their premature beauty for the faded hues of premature old age.

The joyous troops of youthful dancers, before ten o'clock arrived, surrendered the floor to the gentlemen and ladies, who, till now, had been merely spectators of the scene, and being resigned into the hands of their nurses and servants in waiting, were carried home, while the assembly-room, now converted into a regular ball-room, rang till long past the "noon of night" with the enlivening music, confusion, and revelry of a complete and crowded rout. Introductions for a partner in the dance were not the "order of the day," or rather of the night. A gentleman had only to single out some lady among the brilliant assemblage, and though a total stranger, solicit the honour of dancing with her. Such self-introductions are of course merely *pro tem.*, and, like fashionable intimacies formed at Saratoga, never after recognised. Still, to a stranger, such absence of all formality is peculiarly pleasant, and, though every face may be new to him, he has the grateful satisfaction of knowing that he can make himself perfectly at home, and form innumerable delightful acquaintances for the evening, provided he chooses to be sociable, and make the most of the enjoyments around him. We left the hall at an early hour on our return to the hotel.

Crowds of mulatto, French and English hack-drivers were besieging the door, shouting in bad French, worse Spanish, and broken English—

"Coachee, massas! jontilhomme ridee!" "Caballeros, voulez vous tomer mé carriage?" "Wooly woo querie to ride sir?" "Fiacre Messieurs!" "By St. Patrick jintilmen—honie, mounseers, woulee voo my asy riding coach?"—et cetera, mingled with execrations, heavy blows, exchanged in the way of friendship, laughter, yells and Indian whoops, composing a "concord of sweet sounds" to be fully appreciated only by those who have heard similar concerts. We, however, effected our escape from these pupils of Jehu, who, ignorant of our country, in a city where all the nations of the earth are represented, wisely addressed us in a Babelic medley of languages, till we were out of hearing.

Returning, as we came through Rues Royale and St. Pierre, past the quarter of the "gens d'armes," we entered Chartres-street, which was now nearly deserted. Proceeding through this dark, narrow street on our way home, meeting now and then an individual pursuing his hasty and solitary way along the echoing pavé, we arrived at the new Exchange alluded to in my first letter, which served the double purpose of gentlemen's public assembly-room and *café*. As we entered from the dimly lighted street, attracted by the lively crowd dispersed throughout the spacious room, our eyes were dazzled by the noon-day brightness shed from innumerable chandeliers. Having lounged through the room, filled with smokers, newspaper-readers, promenaders, drinkers, &c. &c., till we were stunned by the noise of the multitude, who were talking in an endless variety of languages, clattering upon the ear at once, and making "confusion worse confounded," my polite friend suggested that we should ascend to "the rooms," as they are termed. As I wished to see every thing in New-Orleans interesting or novel to a northerner, I readily embraced the opportunity of an introduction into the penetralium of one of the far-famed temples which the goddess of fortune has erected in this, her favourite city. We ascended a broad flight of steps, one side of which exhibited many lofty double doors, thrown wide open, discovering to our view an extensive hall, in which stood several billiard tables, surrounded by their "mace and cue" devotees.

But as my letter is now of rather an uncharitable length, I will defer till my next, farther description of the deeds and mysteries and unhallowed sacrifices connected with these altars of dissipation.

FOOTNOTE

[4] There is at the North a general misconception of the term "Creole." A friend of mine who had visited

Louisiana for his health, after a residence of a few months gained the affections of a very lovely girl, and married her. He wrote to his uncle in Massachusetts, to whose large estate he was heir-expectant, communicating the event, saying that he "had just been united to an amiable *Creole,* whom he anticipated the pleasure of introducing to him in the Spring." The old gentleman, on receiving the letter, stamped, raved, and swore; and on the same evening replied to his nephew, saying, that as he had disgraced his family by marrying a *Mulatto,* he might remain where he was, as he wished to have nothing to do with him, or any of his woolly-headed, yellow skinned brats, that might be, henceforward." My friend, however, ventured home, and when the old gentleman beheld his lovely bride, he exclaimed, "The d—l, nephew, if you call this little angel a *Creole,* what likely chaps the real ebony Congos must be in that country." The old gentleman is not alone in his conception of a *Creole*. Where there is one individual in New England correctly informed, there are one hundred who, like him, know no distinction between the terms *Creole* and *Mulatto*. "Creole" is simply a synonym for "native." It has, however, only a local, whereas "native" has a general application. To say "He is a *Creole* of Louisiana," is to say "He is a *native* of Louisiana." Contrary to the general opinion at the North, it is seldom applied to coloured persons, *Creole* is sometimes, though not frequently, applied to Mississippians; but with the exception of the West-India Islands, it is usually confined to Louisiana.

XII

My last letter left me on my way up to "the rooms" over the Exchange, where the goddess of fortune sits enthroned, with a "cue" for her sceptre, and a card pack for her "magna charta," dispensing alternate happiness and misery to the infatuated votaries who crowd in multitudes around her altars. Proceeding along the corridor, we left the billiard-room on our left, in which no sound was heard (though every richly-carved, green-covered table was surrounded by players, while numerous spectators reclined on sofas or settees around the room) save the sharp *teck! teck!* of the balls as they came in contact with each other, and the rattling occasioned by the "markers" as they noted the progress of the game on the large parti-coloured "rosaries" extended over the centre of the tables. Lingering here but a moment, we turned an angle of the gallery, and at the farther extremity came to a glass door curtained on the inner side, so as effectually to prevent all observation of the interior. Entering this,—for New-Orleans,—so carefully guarded room, we beheld a scene, which, to an uninitiated, ultra city-bred northerner, would be both novel and interesting.

The first noise which struck our ears on entering, was the clear ringing and clinking of silver, mingled with the technical cries of the gamblers, of "all set"—"seven red"—"few cards"—"ten black," &c.—the eager exclamations of joy or disappointment by the players, and the incessant clattering of the little ivory ball racing its endless round in the roulette-table. On one side of the room was a faro-table, and on the opposite side a roulette. We approached the former, which was thronged on three sides with players, while on the other, toward the wall, was seated the dealer of the game—the "gentleman professeur." He was a portly, respectable looking, jolly-faced Frenchman, with so little of the "black-leg" character stamped upon his physiognomy, that one would be far from suspecting him to be a gambler by profession. This is a profession difficult to be conceived as the permanent and only pursuit of an individual. Your conception of it has probably been taken, as in my own case, from the fashionable novels of the day; and perhaps you have regarded the character as merely the creation of an author's brain, and "the profession" *as* a profession, existing nowhere in the various scenes and circumstances of life.

There are in this city a very great number of these *infernos*, (*anglicè* "hells") all of which—with the exception of a few private ones, resorted to by those gentlemen who may have some regard for appearances—are open from twelve at noon till two in the morning, and thronged by all classes, from the lowest blackguard upward. They are situated in the most public streets, and in the most conspicuous locations. Each house has a bank, as the amount of funds owned by it is termed. Some of the houses have on hand twenty thousand dollars in specie; and when likely to be hard run by heavy losses, can draw for three or four times that amount upon the directors of the "bank company." The establishing of one of these banks is effected much as that of any other. Shares are sold, and many respectable moneyed men, I am informed, become stockholders; though not ambitious, I believe, to have their names made public. It is some of the best stock in the city, often returning an enormous dividend. They are regularly licensed, and pay into the state or city treasury, I forget which, annually more than sixty thousand dollars. From six to twelve well-dressed, genteel looking individuals, are always to be found in attendance, to whom salaries are regularly paid by the directors; and to this salary, and this occupation, they look for as permanent a support through life as do members of any other profession. It is this class of men who are emphatically denominated "gamblers and black legs." The majority of them are Frenchmen, though they usually speak both French and English. Individuals, allured by the hope of winning, are constantly passing in and out of these houses, in "broad noon," with the same indifference to what is termed "public opinion," as they would feel were they going into or out of a store.

Those places which are situated in the vicinity of Canal-street and along the Levée, are generally of a lower order, and thronged with the *canaille* of the city, sailors, Kentucky boatmen, crews of steamboats, and poor Gallic gentlemen, in threadbare long-skirted coats and huge whiskers. The room we were now visiting was of a somewhat higher order, though not exclusively devoted to the more genteel adventurers, as, in the very nature of the thing, such an exclusion would be impossible. But if unruly persons intrude, and are disposed to be obstreperous, the conductors of the rooms, of course, have the power of expelling them at pleasure.

Being merely spectators of the game, we managed to obtain an advantageous position for viewing it, from a vacant settee placed by the side of the portly dealer, who occupied, as his exclusive right, one side of the large table. Before him were placed in two rows thirteen cards; the odd thirteenth capping the double file, like a militia captain at the head of his company, when marching "two by two;" the files of cards, however, unlike these martial files of men, are *straight*. You will readily see by the number, that these cards represent every variety in a pack. The dealer, in addition, has a complete pack, fitting closely in a silver box, from which, by the action of a sliding lid, he adroitly and accurately turns off the cards in dealing. The players, or "betters," as they are termed, place their money in various positions as it respects the thirteen cards upon the table, putting it either on a single card or between two, as their skill, judgment, or fancy may dictate.

As I took my station near the faro-board, the dealer was just shuffling the cards for a new game. There were eleven persons clustered around the table, and as the game was about to commence, arm after arm was reached forth to the prostrate cards, depositing one, five, ten, twenty, or fifty dollars, according to the faith or depth of purse of their owners. On, around, and between the cards, dollars were strewed singly or in piles, while the eyes of every better were fixed immoveably, and, as the game went on, with a painful intensity, upon his own deposit, perhaps his last stake. When the stakes were all laid, the dealer announced it by drawling out in bad English, "all saat." Then, damping his forefinger and thumb, by a summary process—not quite so elegant as common—he began drawing off the cards in succession. The card taken off does not count in the game; the betters all looking to the one turned up in the box to read the fate of their stakes. As the cards are turned, the winners are paid, the money won by the bank swept off with a long wand into the reservoir by the side of the banker, and down go new stakes, doubled or lessened according to the success of the winners—again is drawled out the mechanical "all set," and the same routine is repeated until long past midnight, while the dealers are relieved every two or three hours by their fellow-partners in the house.

At the right hand of the dealer, upon the table, is placed what is denominated "the bank," though it is merely its representative. This is a shallow, yet heavy metal box, about twenty inches long, half as many wide, and two deep, with a strong network of wire, so constructed as to cover the box like a lid, and be secured by a lock. Casting my eye into this receptacle through its latticed top, I noticed several layers of U.S. bank notes, from five to five hundred dollars, which were kept down by pieces of gold laid upon each pile. About one-fifth of the case was parted off from the rest, in which were a very large number of gold ounces and rouleaus of guineas. The whole amount contained in it, so far as I could judge, was about six thousand dollars, while there was more than three thousand dollars in silver, piled openly and most temptingly upon the table around the case, in dollars, halves, and quarters, ready for immediate use. From policy, five franc pieces are substituted for dollars in playing; but the winner of any number of them can, when he ceases playing, immediately exchange them at the bank for an equal number of dollars. It often happens that players, either from ignorance or carelessness, leave the rooms with the five franc pieces; but should they, five minutes afterward, discover their neglect and return to exchange them, the dealer exclaims with an air of surprise—

"Saar! it will be one mistake, saar. I nevair look you in de fas before, saar!" Thousands of dollars are got off annually in this manner, and a very pretty interest the banks derive from their ingenious method of *franking*.

Having seen some thousands of dollars change hands in the course of an hour, and, with feelings somewhat allied to pity, marked the expression of despair, darkening the features of the unfortunate loser, as he rushed from the room with clenched hands and bent brow, muttering indistinctly within his teeth fierce curses upon his luck; and observed, with no sympathizing sensations of pleasure, the satisfaction with which the winners hugged within their arms their piles of silver, we turned from the faro, and crossed the room to the roulette table. These two tables are as inseparable as the shark and the pilot fish, being always found together in every gambling room, ready to make prey of all who come within their influence. At faro there is no betting less than a dollar; here, stakes as low as a quarter are permitted. The players were more numerous at this table than at the former, and generally less genteel in their appearance. The roulette table is a large, long, green-covered board or platform, in the centre of which, placed horizontally upon a pivot, is a richly plated round mahogany table, or wheel, often inlaid with ivory and pearl, and elaborately carved, about two feet in diameter, with the bottom closed like an inverted box cover. Around this wheel, on the inner border, on alternate little black and red squares, are marked numbers as high as thirty-six, with two squares additional, in one a single cipher, in the other two ciphers; while on the green cloth-covered board, the same numbers are marked in squares. The dealer, who occupies one side of the table, with his metal, latticed case of bank notes and gold at his right hand, and piles of silver before him, sets the wheel revolving rapidly, and adroitly spins into it from the end of his thumb, as a boy would snap a marble, an ivory ball, one quarter the size of a billiard ball. The betters, at the same instant, place their money upon such one of the figures drawn upon the cloth as they fancy the most likely to favour them, and intently watch the ball as it races round within the revolving wheel. When the wheel stops, the ball necessarily rests upon some one of the figures in the wheel, and the fortunate player, whose stake is upon the corresponding number on the cloth, is immediately paid his winning, while the stakes of the losers are coolly transferred by the dealer to the constantly accumulating heap before him; again the wheel is set revolving, the little ball rattles around it, and purses are again made lighter and the bank increased.

As we were about to depart, I noticed in an interior room a table spread for nearly a dozen persons, and loaded with all the substantials for a hearty supper. The dealers, or conductors of the bank, are almost all bachelors, I believe, or ought to be, and keep "hall" accordingly, in the same building where lies their theatre of action, in the most independent and uproarious style. After the rooms are closed, which is at about two in the morning, they retire to their supper table, inviting all the betters, both winners and losers, who are present when the playing breaks up, to partake with them. The invitations are generally accepted; and those poor devils who in the course of the evening have been so unfortunate as to have "pockets to let," have at least the satisfaction of enjoying a good repast, *gratis*, before they go home and hang themselves.[5]

Having satisfied our curiosity with a visit to this notable place, we descended into the Exchange, which was now nearly deserted; a few gentlemen only were taking their "night caps" at the bar, and here and there, through the vast room, a solitary individual was pacing backward and forward with echoing footsteps.

Leaving the now deserted hall, which at an earlier hour had resounded with the loud and confused murmur of a hundred tongues, and the tramping of a busy multitude, we proceeded to our hotel through the silent and dimly lighted streets,[6] without being assassinated, robbed, seized by the "*gens d'armes*," and locked up in the guard-house, or meeting any other adventure or misadventure whatever; whereat we were almost tempted to be surprised, remembering the frightful descriptions given by veracious letter-writers, of this "terrible city" of New-Orleans.

FOOTNOTES

[5] Exertions have been made from time to time by the citizens of Louisiana for the suppression of gambling, but their efforts have until recently, been unavailing. During the last session of the legislature of Louisiana, however, a bill to suppress gambling-houses in New-Orleans, passed both houses, and has become a law. One of the enactments provides that the owners or occupants of houses in which gambling is detected, are liable to the penalties of the law. For the first offence, a fine of from one to five thousand dollars; for the second, from ten to fifteen thousand, and confinement in the penitentiary from one to five years, at the discretion of the court. Fines are also imposed for playing at any public gaming

table, or any banking game. The owners of houses where gaming tables are kept, are liable for the penalty, if not collected of the keeper; unless they are able to show that the crime was committed so privately that the owner could not know of it. It also provides for the recovery of any sums of money lost by gaming.

To make up the deficiency in the revenue arising from the abolition of gaming-houses, a bill has been introduced into the legislature providing for the imposition of a tax on all passengers arriving at, or leaving New-Orleans, by ships or steamboats.

[6]Since the above paragraph was penned, the huge swinging lamps have been superseded by gas lights, which now brilliantly illuminate all the principal streets of the city.

XIII

At the commendable hour of one in the morning, as was hinted in my last letter, we safely arrived at our hotel, and roused the slumbering porter from his elysian dreams by the tinkling of a little bell pendant over the private door for "single gentlemen,—*belated;*" and ascended through dark passages and darker stairways to our rooms, lighted by the glimmer of a solitary candle fluttering and flickering by his motion, in the fingers of the drowsy "guardian of doors," who preceded us.

We had finished our late supper, and, toasting our bootless feet upon the burnished fender, were quietly enjoying the agreeable warmth of the glowing coals, and relishing, with that peculiar zest which none but a smoker knows, a real Habana,—when we were suddenly startled from our enjoyment by the thrilling, fearful cry, of "Fire! fire!" which, heard in the silence of midnight, makes a man's heart leap into his throat, while he springs from his couch, as if the cry "To arms—to arms!" had broken suddenly upon his slumbers. "Fire! fire! fire!" rang in loud notes through the long halls and corridors of the spacious hotel, startling the affrighted sleepers from their beds, and at the same instant a fierce, red glare flashed through our curtained windows. The alarm was borne loudly and wildly along the streets—the rapid clattering of footsteps, as some individual hastened by to the scene of the disaster, followed by another, and another, was in a few seconds succeeded by the loud, confused, and hurried tramping of many men, as they rushed along shouting with hoarse voices the quick note of alarm. We had already sprung to the balcony upon which the window of our room opened. For a moment our eyes were dazzled by the fearful splendour of the scene which burst upon us. The whole street,—lofty buildings, towers, and cupolas—reflected a wild, red glare, flashed upon them from a stupendous body of flame, as it rushed and roared, and flung itself toward the skies, which, black, lowering, and gloomy, hung threateningly above. Two of those mammoth steamers which float upon the mighty Mississippi, were, with nearly two thousand bales of cotton on board, wrapped in sheets of fire. They lay directly at the foot of Canal-street; and as the flames shot now and then high in the air, leaping from their decks as though instinct with life, this broad street to its remotest extremity in the distant forests, became lurid with a fitful reddish glare, which disclosed every object with the clearness of day. The balconies, galleries, and windows, were filled with interested spectators; and every street and avenue poured forth its hundreds, who thundered by toward the scene of conflagration. I have a mania for going to fires. I love their blood-stirring excitement; and, as in an engagement, the greater the tumult and danger, the greater is the enjoyment. I do not, however, carry my "incendiary passion" so far as to be vexed because an alarm that turns me out of a warm bed proves to be only a "false alarm," but when a fire does come in my way, I heartily enjoy the excitement necessarily attendant upon the exertions made to extinguish it. You will not be surprised, then, that although I had not had "sleep to my eyes, nor slumber to my eyelids," I should be unwilling to remain a passive and distant spectator of a scene so full of interest. Our hotel was a quarter of a mile from the fire, and yet the heat was sensibly felt at that distance. Leaving my companion to take his rest, I descended to the street, and falling into the tumultuous current setting toward the burning vessels, a few moments brought me to the spacious platform, or wharf, in front of the Levée, which was crowded with human beings, gazing passively upon the fire; while the ruddy glare reflected from their faces, gave them the appearance, so far as complexion was concerned, of so many red men of the forest. As I elbowed my way through this dense mass of people, who were shivering, notwithstanding their proximity to the fire, in the chilly morning air, with one side half roasted, and the other half chilled—the ejaculations—

"Sacré diable!" "Carramba!" "Marie, mon Dieu!" "Mine Got vat a fire!" "By dad, an its mighty waarm"—"Well now the way that ar' cotton goes, is a sin to Crockett!"—fell upon the ear, with a hundred more, in almost every *patois* and dialect, whereof the chronicles of grammar have made light or honourable mention.

As I gained the front of this mass of human beings, that activity which most men possess, who are not modelled after "fat Jack," enabled me to gain an elevation whence I had an unobstructed view of the whole scene of conflagration. The steamers were lying side by side at the Levée, and one of them was enveloped in wreaths of flame, bursting from a thousand cotton bales, which were piled, tier above tier, upon her decks. The inside boat, though having no cotton on board, was rapidly consuming, as the huge streams of fire lapped and twined around her. The night was perfectly calm, but a strong whirlwind had been created by the action of the heat upon the atmosphere, and now and then it swept down in its invisible power, with the "noise of a rushing mighty wind," and as the huge serpentine flames darted upward, the solid cotton bales would be borne round the tremendous vortex like feathers, and then—hurled away into the air, blazing like giant meteors—would descend heavily and rapidly into the dark bosom of the river. The next moment they would rise and float upon the surface, black unshapely masses of tinder. As tier after tier, bursting with fire, fell in upon the burning decks, the sweltering flames, for a moment smothered, preceded by a volcanic discharge of ashes, which fell in showers upon the gaping spectators, would break from their confinement, and darting upward with multitudinous large wads of cotton, shoot them away through the air, filling the sky for a moment with a host of flaming balls. Some of them were borne a great distance through the air, and falling lightly upon the surface of the water, floated, from their buoyancy, a long time unextinguished. The river became studded with fire, and as far as the eye could reach below the city, it presented one of the most magnificent, yet awful spectacles, I had ever beheld or imagined. Literally spangled with flame, those burning fragments in the distance being diminished to specks of light, it had the appearance, though far more dazzling and brilliant, of the starry firmament. There were but two miserable engines to play with this gambolling monster, which, one moment lifting itself to a great height in the air, in huge spiral wreaths, like some immense snake, at the next would contract itself within its glowing furnace, or coil and dart along the decks like troops of fiery serpents, and with the roaring noise of a volcano.

There are but few "fires" in New-Orleans, compared with the great number that annually occur in northern cities. This is owing, not wholly to the universally prevalent style of building with brick, but in a great measure to the very few fires requisite for a dwelling house in a climate so warm as this. Consequently there is much less interest taken by the citizens in providing against accidents of this kind, than would be felt were conflagrations more frequent. The miserably manned engines now acting at intervals upon the fire, presented a very true exemplification of the general apathy. To a New-Yorker or Bostonian, accustomed to the activity, energy, and military precision of their deservedly celebrated fire companies, the mob-like disorder of those who pretended to work the engines at this fire, would create a smile, and suggest something like the idea of a caricature.

After an hour's toil by the undisciplined firemen, assisted by those who felt disposed to aid in extinguishing the flame, the fire was got under, but not before one of the boats was wholly consumed, with its valuable cargo. The inner boat was saved from total destruction by the great exertions of some few individuals, "who fought on their own hook."

The next morning I visited the scene of the disaster. Thousands were gathered around, looking as steadily and curiously upon the smouldering ruins as if they had possessed some very peculiar and interesting attraction. The river presented a most lively scene. A hundred skiffs, wherries, punts, dug-outs, and other non-descript craft, with equally euphonic denominations, were darting about in all directions, each propelled by one or two individuals, who were gathering up the half saturated masses of cotton, that whitened the surface of the river as far as the eye could reach. Several unlucky wights, in their ambitious eagerness to obtain the largest piles of this "snow-drift," would lose their equilibrium, and tumble headlong with their wealth of cotton into the water. None of them, however, were drowned, their mishaps rather exciting the merriment of their companions and of the crowds of amused spectators on shore, than creating any apprehensions for their safety.

The misfortune of one shrivelled-up old Portuguese, who had been very active in securing a due proportion of the cotton, occasioned no little laughter among the crowd on the Levée. After much fighting, quarreling, and snarling, he had filled his little boat so completely, that his thin, black, hatchet-face, could only be seen protruding above the snowy mass in which he was imbedded. Seizing his oars in his long bony hands, he began to pull for the shore with his prize, when a light wreath of blue smoke rose from the cotton and curled very ominously over his head. All unconscious, he rowed on, and before he gained the shore, the fire burst in a dozen places at once from his combustible cargo, and instantly enveloped the little man and his boat in a bright sheet of flame; with a terrific yell he threw himself into the water, and in a few moments emerged close by the Levée, where he was picked up, with no other personal detriment than the loss of the little forelock of gray hair which time had charitably spared him.

In one instance, two skiffs, with a single individual in each, attracted attention by racing for a large tempting float of cotton, which drifted along at some distance in the stream. Shouts of encouragement rose from the multitude as they watched the competitors, with the interest similar to that felt upon a race-course. The light boats flew over the water like arrows on the wing. They arrived at the same instant at the object of contest, one on either side, and the occupants, seizing it simultaneously, and without checking the speed of their boats, bore the mass of cotton through the water between them, ploughing and tossing the spray in showers over their heads. Gradually the boats stopped, and a contest of another kind began. Neither would resign his prize. After they had remained leaning over the sides of their boats for a moment, grasping it and fiercely eyeing each other, some words were apparently exchanged between them, for they mutually released their hold upon the cotton, brought their boats together and secured them; then, stripping off their roundabouts, placed themselves on the thwarts of their boats in a pugilistic attitude, and prepared to decide the ownership of the prize, by an appeal to the "law of *arms*." The other cotton-hunters desisted from their employment, and seizing their oars, pulled with shouts to the scene of contest. Before they reached it, the case had been decided, and the foremost of the approaching boatmen had the merit of picking from the water the conquered hero, who, after gallantly giving and taking a dozen fine rounds, received an unlucky "settler" under the left ear, whereupon he tumbled over the side, and was fast sinking, when he was taken out, amid the shouts of the gratified spectators, with his hot blood effectually cooled, though not otherwise injured. The more fortunate victor deliberately lifted the prize into the boat, and fixing a portion on the extremity of an oar, set it upright, and rowed to shore amid the cheers and congratulations of his fellows, who now assembling in a fleet around him, escorted him in triumph.

XIV

Canal-street, as I have in a former letter observed, with its triple row of young sycamores, extending throughout the whole length, is one of the most spacious, and destined at no distant period, to be one of the first and handsomest streets in the city. Every building in the street is of modern construction, and some blocks of its brick edifices will vie in tasteful elegance with the boasted granite piles of Boston.

Yesterday, after a late dinner, the afternoon being very fine, I left my hotel, and without any definite object in view, strolled up this street. The first object which struck me as worthy of notice was a small brick octagon church, enclosed by a white paling, on the corner of Bourbon-street. The entrance was overgrown with long grass, and the footsteps of a worshipper seemed not to have pressed its threshold for many an unheeded Sunday. In its lonely and neglected appearance, there was a silent but forcible comment upon that censurable neglect of the Sabbath, which, it has been said, prevails too generally among the citizens of New-Orleans. In front of this church, which is owned, I believe, by the Episcopalians, stands a white marble monument, surmounted by an urn, erected in memory of the late Governor Claiborne. With this solitary exception, there are no public monuments in this city. For a city so ancient, (that is, with reference to cis-Atlantic antiquity) as New-Orleans, and so French in its tastes and habits, I am surprised at this; as the French themselves have as great a mania for triumphal arches, statues, and public monuments, as had the ancient Romans. But this fancy they seem not to have imported among their other nationalities; or, perhaps, they have not found occasions for its frequent exercise.

The government house, situated diagonally opposite to the church, and retired from the street, next attracted my attention. It was formerly a hospital, but its lofty and spacious rooms are now convened into public offices. Its snow-white front, though plain, is very imposing; and the whole structure, with its handsome, detached wings, and large green, thickly covered with shrubbery in front, luxuriant with orange and lemon trees, presents, decidedly, one of the finest views to be met with in the city. These two buildings, with the exception of some elegant private residences, are all that are worth remarking in this street, which, less than a mile from the river, terminates in the swampy commons, every where surrounding New-Orleans, except on the river side.

Not far beyond the government house, the Mall, which ornaments the centre of Canal-street, forms a right angle, and extends down Rampart-street to Esplanade-street, and there making another right angle, extends back again to the river, nearly surrounding the "city proper" with a triple row of sycamores, which, in the course of a quarter of a century, for grandeur, beauty, and convenience, will be without a parallel. The city of New-Orleans is planned on a magnificent scale, happily and judiciously combining ornament and convenience. Let the same spirit which foresaw and provided for its present greatness, animate those who will hereafter direct its public improvements, and New-Orleans, in spite of its bug-bear character and its unhealthy location, will eventually be the handsomest, if not the largest city in the United States.

Following the turning of the Mall, I entered Rampart-street, which, with its French and Spanish buildings, presented quite a contrast to the New-England-like appearance of that I had just quitted. There are some fine buildings at the entrance of this street, which is not less broad than the former. On the right I passed a small edifice, much resembling a Methodist meeting-house, such as are seen in northern villages, which a passing Frenchman, lank and tall, in answer to my inquiry, informed me was "L'eglise Evangelique, Monsieur," with a touch of his chapeau, and a wondrous evolution of his attenuated person. This little church was as neglected, and apparently unvisited as its episcopalian neighbour. A decayed, once-white paling surrounded it; but the narrow gate, in front of the edifice, probably constructed to be opened and shut by devout hands, was now secured by a nail, whose red coat of rust indicated long and peaceable possession of its present station over the latch. Comment again, thought I, as I passed on down the street, to where I had observed, not far distant, a crowd gathered around the door of a large white-stuccoed building, burthened by a clumsy hunch-backed kind of tower, surmounted by a huge wooden cross.

On approaching nearer, I discovered many carriages extended in a long line up the street, and a hearse with tall black plumes, before the door of the building, which, I was informed, was the Catholic chapel. Passing through the crowd around the entrance, I gained the portico, where I had a full view of the interior, and the ceremony then in progress. In the centre of the chapel, in which was neither pew nor seat, elevated upon a high frame or altar, over which was thrown a black velvet pall, was placed a coffin, covered also with black velvet. A dozen huge wax candles, nearly as long and as large as a ship's royal-mast, standing in candlesticks five feet high, burned around the corpse, mingled with innumerable candles of the ordinary size, which were thickly sprinkled among them, like lesser stars, amid the twilight gloom of the chapel. The mourners formed a lane from the altar to the door, each holding a long, unlighted, wax taper, tipped at the larger end with red, and ornamented with fanciful paper cuttings. Around the door, and along the sides of the chapel, stood casual spectators, strangers, and negro servants without number. As I entered, several priests and singing-boys, in the black and white robes of their order, were chanting the service for the dead. The effect was solemn and impressive. In a few moments the ceremony was completed, and four gentlemen, dressed in deep mourning, each with a long white scarf, extending from one shoulder across the breast, and nearly to the feet, advanced, and taking the coffin from its station, bore it through the line of mourners, who fell in, two and two behind them, to the hearse, which immediately moved on to the grave-yard with its burthen, followed by the carriages, as in succession they drove up to the chapel, and received the mourners. The last carriage had not left the door, when a man, followed by two little girls, entered from the back of the chapel, and commenced extinguishing the lights:—he, with an extinguisher, much resembling in size and shape an ordinary funnel, affixed to the extremity of a rod ten feet long, attacking the larger ones, while his youthful coadjutors operated with the forefinger and thumb upon the others. In a few moments every light, except two or three, was extinguished, and the "Chapel of the Dead" became silent and deserted.

To this chapel the Roman Catholic dead are usually brought before burial, to receive the last holy office, which, saving the rite of sepulture, the living can perform for the dead. These chapels are the last resting-places of their bodies, before they are consigned for ever to the repose of the grave. To every Catholic then, among all temples of worship, these chapels—his *last home* among the dwelling-places of men—must be objects of peculiar sanctity and veneration.

Burial-grounds, even in the humblest villages, are always interesting to a stranger. They are marble chronicles of the past; where, after studying the lively characters around him, he can retire, and over a page that knows no flattery, hold communion with the dead.

The proposition that "care for the dead keeps pace with civilization" is, generally, true.—The more refined and cultivated are a people, the more attention they pay to the performance of the last offices for the departed. The citizens of the United States will not certainly acknowledge themselves second to any nation in point of refinement. But look at their cemeteries. Most of them crown some bleak hill, or occupy the ill-fenced corners of some barren and treeless common, overrun by cattle, whose preference for the long luxuriant grass, suffered to grow there by a kind of prescriptive right, is matter of general observation. Our neglect of the dead is both a reproach and a proverb. Look at England; every village there has its rural burying-ground, which on Sundays is filled with the well-dressed citizens and villagers, who walk among the green graves of parents, children, or friends, deriving from their reflections the most solemn and impressive lesson the human heart can learn. In America, on the contrary, the footsteps of a solitary individual, the slow and heavy tramp of a funeral procession, or the sacrilegious intrusion of idle school-boys—who approach a grave but to deface its marble—are the only disturbers of the graveyard's loneliness.

But even England is behind France. There every tomb-stone is crowned with a chaplet of roses, and every grave is a variegated bed of flowers. Spain, dark and gloomy Spain! is behind all. Whoever has rambled among her gloomy cemeteries, or gazed with feelings of disgust and horror, upon the pyramids of human sculls, bleaching in those Golgothas, the *Campos santos* of Monte Video, Buenos Ayres, and South America generally, need not be reminded how little they venerate what once moved—the image of God! The Italians singularly unite the indifference of the Spaniards with the affection of the French in their respect for the dead. Compare the "dead vaults" of Italia's cities, with the pleasant cemeteries in her green vales! Without individualising the European nations, I will advert to the Turks, who, though not the most refined, are a sensitive and reflecting people, and pay great honours to their departed friends, as the mighty "City of the Dead" which encompasses Constantinople evinces. But the cause of this respect is to be traced, rather to their Moslem creed, than to the intellectual character, or refinement of the people.

To what is to be attributed the universal indifference of Americans to honouring the dead, by those little mementos and marks of affection and respect which are interwoven with the very religion of other countries? There are not fifty burial-grounds throughout the whole extent of the Union, which can be termed beautiful, rural, or even neat. The Bostonians, in the possession of their lonely and romantic Mount Auburn, have redeemed their character from the almost universal charge of apathy and indifference manifested by their fellow countrymen upon this subject. Next to Mount Auburn, the cemetery in New-Haven is the most beautifully picturesque of any in this country. In Maine there is but one, the burial-place in Brunswick, deserving of notice. Its snow-white monuments glance here and there in bold relief among the dark melancholy pines which overshadow it, casting a funereal gloom among its deep recesses, particularly appropriate to the sacred character of the spot.

I intended to devote this letter to a description of my visit to the Roman Catholic burying-ground of this city, the contemplation of which has given occasion to the preceding remarks, and from which I have just returned; but I have rambled so far and so long in my digression, that I shall have scarcely time or room to express all I intended in this sheet. But that I need not encroach with the subject upon my next, I will complete my remarks here, even at the risk of subjecting myself to—with *me*—the unusual charge of *brevity*.

Leaving the chapel, I followed the procession which I have described, for at least three quarters of a mile down a long street or road at right angles with Rampart-street, to the place of interment. The priests and boys, who in their black and white robes had performed the service for the dead, leaving the chapel by a private door in the rear of the building, made their appearance in the street leading to the cemetery, as the funeral train passed down, each with a black mitred cap upon his head, and there forming into a procession upon the side walk, they moved off in a course opposite to the one taken by the funeral train, and soon disappeared in the direction of the cathedral. Two priests, however, remained with the procession, and with it, after passing on the left hand the "old Catholic cemetery," which being full, to repletion is closed and sealed for the "Great Day," arrived at the new burial-place. Here the mourners alighted from their carriages, and proceeded on foot to the tomb. The priests, bare-headed and solemn, were the last who entered, except myself and a few other strangers attracted by curiosity.

This cemetery is quite out of the city; there being no dwelling or enclosure of any kind beyond it. On approaching it, the front on the street presents the appearance of a lofty brick wall of very great length, with a spacious gateway in the centre. This gateway is about ten feet deep; and one passing through it, would imagine the wall of the same solid thickness. This however is only apparent. The wall which surrounds, or is to surround the four sides of the burial-ground, (for it is yet uncompleted,) is about twelve feet in height, and ten in thickness. The external appearance on the street is similar to that of any other high wall, while to a beholder within, the cemetery exhibits three stories of oven-like tombs, constructed *in* the wall, and extending on every side of the grave-yard. Each of these tombs is designed to admit only a single coffin, which is enclosed in the vault with masonry, and designated by a small marble slab fastened in the face of the wall at the head of the coffin, stating the name, age, and sex of the deceased. By a casual estimate I judged there were about eighteen hundred apertures in this vast pile of tombs. This method, resorted to here from necessity, on account of the nature of the soil, might serve as a hint to city land-economists.

When I entered the gateway, I was struck with surprise and admiration. Though destitute of trees, the cemetery is certainly more deserving, from its peculiarly novel and unique appearance, of the attention of strangers, than (with the exception of that at New-Haven, and Mount Auburn,) any other in the United States. From the entrance to the opposite side through the centre of the grave-yard, a broad avenue or street extends nearly an eighth of a mile in length; and on either side of this are innumerable isolated tombs, of all sizes, shapes, and descriptions, built above ground. The idea of a Lilliputian city was at first suggested to my mind on looking down this extensive avenue. The tombs in their various and fantastic styles of architecture—if I may apply the term to these tiny edifices— resembled cathedrals with towers, Moorish dwellings, temples, chapels, palaces, *mosques*—substituting the cross for the crescent—and structures of almost every kind. The idea was ludicrous enough; but as I passed down the avenue, I could not but indulge the fancy that I was striding down the Broadway of the capital of the Lilliputians. I mention this, not irreverently, but to give you the best idea I can of the cemetery, from my own impressions. Many of the tombs were constructed like, and several were, indeed, miniature Grecian temples; while others resembled French, or Spanish edifices, like those found in "old Castile." Many of them, otherwise plain, were surmounted by a tower supporting a cross. All were perfectly white, arranged with the most perfect regularity, and distant little more than a foot from each other. At the distance of every ten rods the main avenue was intersected by others of less width, crossing it at right angles, down which tombs were ranged in the same novel and regular manner. The whole cemetery was divided into squares, formed by these narrow streets intersecting the principal avenue. It was in reality a "City of the Dead." But it was a city composed of miniature palaces, and still more diminutive villas.

The procession, after passing two-thirds of the way up the spacious walk, turned down one of the narrower alleys, where a new tomb, built on a line with the others, gaped wide to receive its destined inmate. The procession stopped. The coffin was let down from the shoulders of the bearers, and rolled on wooden cylinders into the tomb. The mourners silently gathered around; every head was bared; and amid the deep silence that succeeded, the calm, clear, melancholy voice of the priest suddenly swelled upon the still evening air, in the plaintive chant of the last service for the dead. "Requiescat in pace!" was slowly chanted by the priest,—repeated in subdued voices by the mourners, and echoing among the tombs, died away in the remotest recesses of the cemetery.

The dead was surrendered to the companionship of the dead—the priest and mourners moved slowly away from the spot, and the silence of the still evening was only broken by the clinking of the careless mason, as he proceeded to wall up the aperture in the tomb.

As night was fast approaching, I hastened to leave the place; and, taking a shorter route than by the principal avenue, I came suddenly upon a desolate area, without a tomb to relieve its dank and muddy surface, dotted with countless mounds, where the bones of the moneyless, friendless stranger lay buried. There was no stone to record their names or country. Fragments of coffins were scattered around, and new-made graves, half filled with water, yawned on every side awaiting their unknown occupants; who, perchance, may now be "laying up store for many years" of anticipated happiness. Such is the nature of the soil here, that it is impossible to dig two feet below the surface without coming to water. The whole land seems to be only a thin crust of earth, of not more than three feet in thickness, floating upon the surface of the water. Consequently, every grave will have two feet or more of water in it, and when a coffin is placed therein, some of the assistants have to stand upon it, and keep it down till the grave is re-filled with the mud which was originally thrown from it, or it would float. The citizens, therefore, having a very natural repugnance to being drowned, after having died a natural death upon their beds, choose to have their last resting-place a dry one; and hence the great number of tombs, and the peculiar features of this burial-place.

Returning, I glanced into the old Catholic cemetery, in the rear of the chapel before alluded to. It was crowded with tombs, though without displaying the systematic arrangement observed in the one I had just left. There is another burying-place, in the upper faubourg, called the Protestant cemetery. Here, as its appellation indicates, are buried all who are not of "Holy Church." There are in it some fine monuments, and many familiar names are recorded upon the tomb-stones. Here moulder the remains of thousands, who, leaving their distant homes, buoyant with all the hopes and visions of youth, have been suddenly cut down under a foreign sun, and in the spring time of life. When present enjoyment seemed prophetic of future happiness, they have found here—a stranger's unmarbled grave! A northerner cannot visit this cemetery, and read the familiar names of the multitudes who have ended their lives in this pestilential climate, without experiencing emotions of the most affecting nature. Here the most promising of our northern young men have found an untimely grave: and, as she long has been, so New-Orleans continues, and will long continue to be, the charnel-house of the pride and nobleness of New-England.

XV

A quondam fellow-student, who has been some months a resident of this city, surprised and gratified me this morning with a call. With what strong—more than brotherly affection, we grasp the hand of an old friend and fellow-toiler in academic groves! No two men ever meet like old classmates a year from college!

After exchanging congratulations, he kindly offered to devote the day to the gratification of my curiosity, and accompany me to all those places invested with interest and novelty in the eye of a stranger, which I had not yet visited.

On my replying in the negative to his inquiry, "If I had visited the railway?" we decided on making that the first object of our attention. Though more than a mile distant, we concluded, as the morning was uncommonly fine, to proceed thither on foot, that we might, on the way, visit the venerable convent of the Ursulines, the old Spanish barracks, and one or two other places of minor interest.

Sallying from our hotel, we crossed to the head of Chartres-street, and threaded our way among the busy multitude, who, moving in all directions, on business or pleasure, thronged its well-paved side-walks. On both sides of the way, for several squares, the buildings were chiefly occupied by wholesale and retail dry goods dealers, who are mostly northerners; so that a Yankee stranger feels himself quite at home among them; but before he reaches the end of the long, narrow street, he might imagine himself again a stranger, in a city of France. The variety of the streets, here, is almost as great as the diversity of character among the people. New-Orleans seems to have been built by a universal subscription, to which every European nation has contributed a street, as it certainly has citizens. From one, which to a Bostonian looks like an old acquaintance, you turn suddenly into another that reminds you of Marseilles. Here a street lined with long, narrow, grated windows, in dingy, massive buildings, surrounded by Moorish turrets, urns, grotesque ornaments of grayish stone and motley arabesque, would bring back to the exiled Castilian the memory of his beloved Madrid. In traversing the next, a Parisian might forget that the broad Atlantic rolled between him and the boasted city of his nativity. Here is one that seems to have been transplanted from the very midst of Naples; while its interesting neighbour reminds one of the quaker-like plainness of Philadelphia. There are not, it is true, many which possess decidedly an individual character; for some of them contain such a heterogeneous congregation of buildings, that one cannot but imagine their occupants, in emigrating from every land under heaven, to have brought their own houses with them. The most usual style of building at present, is after the Boston school—if I may so term the fashion of the plain, solid, handsome brick and granite edifices, which are in progress here, as well as in every other city in the union; a style of architecture which owes its origin to the substantial good taste of the citizens of the goodly "city of notions." The majority of structures in the old, or French section of New-Orleans, are after the Spanish and French orders. This style of building is not only permanent and handsome, but peculiarly adapted, with its cool, paved courts, lofty ceilings, and spacious windows, to this sultry climate; and I regret that it is going rapidly out of fashion. Dwellings of this construction have, running through their centre, a broad, high-arched passage, with huge folding-doors, or gates, leading from the street to a paved court in the rear, which is usually surrounded by the sleeping-rooms and offices, communicating with each other by galleries running down the whole square. In the centre of this court usually stands a cistern, and placed around it, in large vases, are flowers and plants of every description. In their love for flowers, the Creoles are truly and especially French. The glimpses one has now and then, in passing through the streets, and by the ever-open doors of the Creoles' residences, of brilliant flowers and luxuriantly blooming exotics, are delightfully refreshing, and almost sufficient to tempt one to a "petit larceny." You may know the residence of a Creole here, even if he resides in a Yankee building, by his mosaic-paved court-yard, filled with vases of flowers.

On arriving at Toulouse-street, which is the fifth intersecting Chartres-street, we turned into it, and pursued our way to the basin, in the rear of the city, which I was anxious to visit. A spectator in this street, on looking toward either extremity, can discover shipping. To the east, the dense forest of masts, bristling on the Mississippi, bounds his view; while, at the west, his eye falls upon the humbler craft, which traverse the sluggish waters of Lake Pontchartrain. This basin will contain about thirty small vessels. There were lying along the pier, when we arrived, five or six miserable-looking sloops and schooners, compared to which, our "down easters" are packet ships. These ply regularly between New-Orleans and Mobile, and by lading and discharging at this point, have given to this retired part of the city quite a business-like and sea-port air. The basin communicates with the lake, four miles distant, by means of a good canal. A mile below the basin, a rail-way has been lately constructed from the Mississippi to the lake, and has already nearly superseded the canal; but of this more anon.

Leaving the basin, we passed a treeless green, which, we were informed by a passer-by, was dignified by the classical appellation of "Congo Square." Here, our obliging informant gave us to understand, the coloured "ladies and gentlemen" are accustomed to assemble on gala and saints' days, and to the time of outlandish music, dance, not the "Romaika," alas! but the "Fandango;" or, wandering in pairs, tell their dusky loves, within the dark shadows, not of jungles or palm groves, but of their own sable countenances. As the Congoese *élite* had not yet left their kitchens, we, of course, had not the pleasure of seeing them move in the mystic dance, upon the "dark fantastic toe," to the dulcet melody of a Congo *banjo*.

From the centre of this square, a fine view of the rear of the Cathedral is obtained, nearly a mile distant, at the head of Orleans-street, which terminates opposite the square. In this part of the town the houses were less compact, most of them of but one story, with steep projecting roofs, and graced by *parterres*; while many of the dwellings were half embowered with the rich green foliage of the fragrant orange and lemon trees. At the corner of rues St. Claude and St. Anne, we passed a very pretty buff-coloured, stuccoed edifice, retired from the street, which we were informed was the Masonic lodge. There are several others, I understand, in various parts of the city. A little farther, on rue St. Claude, in a lonely field, is a small plain building, denominated the College of Orleans, which has yet obtained no literary celebrity. Opposite to this edifice is the foot of Ursuline-street, up which we turned, in our ramble over the city, and proceeded toward the river. It may appear odd to you, that we should *ascend* to the river; but such is the case here. You are aware, from the descriptions in one of my former letters, that the surface of the Mississippi, at its highest tide, is several feet higher than the surrounding country; and that it is restrained from wholly inundating it, only by banks, or *levées*, constructed at low stages of the water. Nowhere is this fact so evident as in New-Orleans. For the purpose of cleansing the city, water is let in at the heads of all those streets which terminate upon the river, by aqueducts constructed through the base of the Levée, and this artificial torrent rushes *from* the river down the gutters, on each side of the streets, with as much velocity as, in other places, it would display in seeking to mingle with the stream. Sometimes the impetus is sufficient to carry the dirty torrents quite across the city into the swamps beyond. But when this is not the case, it must remain in the deep drains and gutters along the side-walks, impregnated with the quintessence of all the filth encountered in its Augean progress, exhaling its noisome effluvia, and poisoning the surrounding atmosphere. All the streets in the back part of the city are bordered on either side with a canal of an inky-coloured, filthy liquid, (water it cannot be termed) from which arises an odour or incense by no means acceptable to the olfactory sensibilities. The streets running parallel with the river, having no inclination either way, are, as a natural consequence of their situation, redolent of these Stygian exhalations. Why New-Orleans is not depopulated to a man, when once the yellow fever breaks out in it, is a miracle. From the peculiarity of its location, and a combination of circumstances, it must always be more or less unhealthy. But were the police, which is at present rather of a military than a civil character, regulated more with a view to promote the comfort and health of the community, the evil might be in a great measure remedied, and many hundred lives annually preserved.

On ascending Ursuline-street, we remarked what I had previously noticed in several other streets, upon the doors of unoccupied dwellings, innumerable placards of "Chambre garnie," "Maison à louer," "Appartement à louer," &c. On inquiry, I ascertained that their former occupants had been swept away by the cholera and yellow fever, which have but a few weeks ceased their ravages. Four out of five houses, which we had seen advertised to let, in different parts of the city, were French, from which I should judge that the majority of the victims were Creoles. The effects of the awful reign of the pestilence over this devoted city, have not yet disappeared. The terrific spirit has passed by, but his lingering shadow still casts a funereal gloom over the theatre of his power. The citizens generally are apparelled in mourning; and the public places of amusement have long been closed.

The old Ursuline convent stands between Ursuline and Hospital streets, and opposite to the barracks, usually denominated the "Old Spanish Barracks." Crossing rue Royale, we first visited those on the south side of Hospital-street. On inquiring of an old, gray-headed soldier, standing in front of a kind of guard-house, if the long, massive pile of brick, which extended from the street more than two hundred feet to the rear, "were the barracks?" he replied, with genuine Irish brogue, "Which barracks, jintlemen?" Ignorant of more than one place of the kind, we repeated the question with emphasis. "Why yes, yer 'onours, its thim same they are, an' bad luck to the likes o' them." We inquired "if the regiment was quartered here?" "The rigiment is it, jintlemen! och, but it's not here at all, at all; divil a rigiment has been in it (the city meaning) this many a month. The sogers, what's come back, is quarthered, ivery mother's son o' them, in the private hoose of a jintleman jist by."

"Why did they leave the city?"

"For fear o' the cholery, sure. But there's a rigiment ixpicted soon, and they'll quarther here, jintlemen; and we're repeerin' the barracks to contain thim, till the new ones is ericted; 'cause these is not the illigant barracks what's goin' to be ericted, sure."

Finding our Milesian so communicative, we questioned him farther, and obtained much interesting information. From the street, the barracks, which are now unoccupied, present the appearance of a huge arcade, formed by a colonnade of massive brick pillars, running along its whole length. Some portion of the front was stuccoed, giving a handsome appearance to that part of the building. The whole is to be finished in the same manner, and when completed, the structure will be a striking ornament to New-Orleans: probably a rival of the "splendid new edifice" about to be erected in a lower part of the city. Though called the "Spanish Barracks," I am informed that they were erected by the Duke of Orleans, when he governed this portion of the French possessions. Immediately opposite to the barracks, in the convent yard, are two very ancient wooden guard-houses, blackened and decayed with age, about thirty feet in height, looking very much like armless windmills, or mammoth pigeon-houses.

The convent next invited our notice. It has, till within a few years, been very celebrated for its school for young ladies, who were sent here from all the southern part of the Union, and even from Europe. A few years since, a new convent was erected two miles below the city, whither the Ursuline ladies have removed; and where they still keep a boarding-school for young ladies, which is highly and justly celebrated. The old building is now occupied by the public schools. Desirous of visiting so fine a specimen of cis-Atlantic antiquity, and at the same time to make some observation of the system of education pursued in this city, we proceeded toward the old gateway of the convent, to apply for admittance.

We might have belaboured the rickety gate till doomsday, without gaining admittance, had not an unlucky, or rather, lucky stroke which we decided should be our last, brought the old wicket rattling about our ears, enveloping us in clouds of dust, as it fell with a tremendous crash upon the pavement. At this very alarming *contre temps*, we had not time to make up our minds whether to beat a retreat, or encounter the assault of an ominously sounding tongue, which thundered "mutterings dire," as with anger in her eye, and wonder in her mien, the owner rushed from a little porter's lodge, which stood on the right hand within the gate,

> "To see what could in nature be the matter,
> To crack her lugs with such a ponderous clatter."

We succeeded in appeasing the ire of the offended janitress, and proceeded across a deserted court covered with short grass, to the principal entrance of the convent, which stands about seventy feet back from the street.

This edifice presents nothing remarkable, except its size, it being about one hundred feet in front, by forty deep. Its aspect is venerable, but extremely plain, the front being entirely destitute of ornament or architectural taste. It is stuccoed, and apparently was once white, but it is now gray with rust and age. It may be called either a French or Spanish building, for it equally evinces both styles of architecture; presenting that anomaly, characteristic of those old structures which give a fine antiquated air to that part of the city. Massive pilasters with heavy cornices, tall, deep windows, huge doorways, and flat roofs, are the distinguishing features of this style of building. Never more than two, the dwellings are usually but one very lofty story in height, and covered with a light yellow stucco, in imitation of dingy-white, rough hewn marble. In internal arrangement and decorations, and external appearance, they differ but little from each other. As we passed under the old, sunken portal, the confused muttering of some hundred treble tongues, mingled, now and then, with a deep bass grumble of authority, burst upon our ears, and intimated our proximity to the place where "young ideas are taught to shoot." Wishing to gratify our curiosity by rambling through the convent's deserted halls and galleries, before we entered the rooms whence the noise proceeded, we ascended a spacious winding stairway; but there was nothing to be seen in the second story, except deserted rooms, and we ascended yet another stair-case to a low room in the attic, formerly the dormitory of the nunnery. While on our return to the first floor, a gentleman, M. Priever, who was, as we afterward ascertained, principal of the public schools of the city, encountered us on the stairs, and politely invited us to visit the different school-rooms within the building. We first accompanied him to the extremity of a long gallery, where he ushered us into a pleasant room, in which a dozen boys were sitting round a table, translating Latin exercises into French. This class, he informed us, he had just taken from the primary school below stairs, to instruct in the elementary classics. From this gentleman we ascertained that there were in the city two primary schools, one within the convent walls, and the other a mile distant, in the northern faubourg. From these two schools, when properly qualified, the pupils are removed into the high, or classic school, kept within the convent. He observed that he had the supervision of these three schools—the high, and two primary—though each had its own particular teacher. The principals of the two convent schools are gentlemen distinguished both for urbanity and literary endowments. In the classical school, pupils can obtain almost every advantage which a collegiate course would confer upon them. The French and Spanish languages form a necessary part of their education; and but few young men resort to northern colleges from New-Orleans. It is the duty of the principal often to visit the primary schools—select from their most promising pupils, those qualified to enter the high school—form them into classes by daily recitations in his own room, (in which employment he was engaged when we entered,) and then pass them over to the teacher of the school they are prepared to enter.

With Mons. P. we visited the classical school, where fifty or sixty young gentlemen were pursuing the higher branches of study. The instructer was a Frenchman, as are all the other teachers. In this, and the other departments, the greater portion of the students also are of French descent; and probably about one-third, in all the schools, are of American parentage. Mons. P. informed me that the latter usually acquired, after being in the school six weeks, or two months, sufficient French for all colloquial purposes. He observed that the majority of the scholars, in all the departments, spoke both languages (French and English,) with great fluency. After hearing two or three classes translate Greek and Latin authors into French, and one or two embryo mathematicians demonstrate Euclid, in the same tongue, we proceeded to the opposite wing of the building, and were ushered into the rattle, clangor, and confusion of the primary department. We were politely received by Mons. Bigot, a Parisian, a fine scholar, and an estimable man. You have visited infant schools for boys, I believe; recall to mind the novel and amusing scenes you there beheld, and you will have an idea of this primary school. The only difference would be, that here the pupils are rough, tearing boys, from fifteen years of age to three. Here, as in the former, they marched and counter-marched, clapped their hands, stamped hard upon the floor, and performed various evolutions for the purpose of circulating the blood, which by sitting too long is apt to stagnate, and render them, particularly in this climate, dull and sleepy. We listened to some of their recitations, which were in the lowest elementary branches, and took our leave under infinite obligations to the politeness and attention of the gentlemanly superintendents.

Besides these, there are private schools for both sexes. The majority of the young ladies are educated by the Ursulines at the convent, in the lower faubourg. Some of the public schools are exclusively for English, and others exclusively for French children. Many pupils are also instructed by private tutors, particularly in the suburbs.

XVI

In a preceding letter, I have alluded to an intended visit to the rail-way; near which, on my way thither, my last letter left me, in company with B., after having paid a visit to the Ursuline convent. On leaving Ursuline-street, which terminates at the river, we proceeded a short distance, to the rail-road, along the Levée, which was lined with ships, bearing the flags of nearly all the nations of the earth. The length of this rail-way is about five miles, terminating at Lake Pontchartrain. Its advantages to New-Orleans are incalculable. It has been to the city literally "an avenue of wealth" already. The trade carried on through this medium, bears no mean proportion to the river commerce. Ports, heretofore unknown to Orleans, as associated with traffic, carry on, now, a regular and important branch of trade with her. By it, a great trade is carried on with Mobile and other places along the Florida coast, and by the same means, the mails are transported with safety and rapidity. The country between New-Orleans and the nearest shore of the lake, is low, flat, marshy, and covered with a half-drowned and stunted forest. The lake, though near the city, formerly was inaccessible. Vessels laden with their valuable cargoes might arrive at the termination of the lake within sight of the city, but the broad marsh extending between them and the far-off towers of the wished-for mart, might as well have been the cloud-capped Jura, for any means of communication it could afford. But the rail-way has overcome this obstacle: coasting vessels, which traverse the lake in great numbers, can now receive and discharge their cargoes at the foot of the rail-way, upon a long pier extending far out into the lake. The discharged cargoes are piled upon the cars and in twenty minutes are added to the thousand shiploads, heaped upon the Levée; or, placed upon drays, are trundling to every part of the city.

When we arrived at the rail-way, the cars for passengers, eight or ten in number, were standing in a line under a long roof, which covers the end of the rail-way. A long train of baggage or cargo-cars were in the rear of these, all heavily laden. The steam-car, puffing and blowing like a bustling little man in a crowd, seemed impatient to dart forward upon the track. We perceived that all was ready for a start; and barely had time to hasten to the ticket-office, throw down our six "bits" for two tickets, and spring into the only vacant seats in one of the cars, before the first bell rang out the signal for starting.

All the cars were full; including two or three behind, appropriated to coloured gentlemen and ladies. Again the bell gave the final signal; and obedient thereto, our fiery leader moved forward, smoking like a race-horse, slowly and steadily at first—then, faster and faster, till we flew along the track with breathless rapidity. The rail-road, commencing at the Levée, runs for the first half mile through the centre of a broad street, with low detached houses on either side. A mile from the Levée we had left the city and all dwellings behind us, and were flying through the fenceless, uninhabited marshes, where nothing meets the eye but dwarf trees, rank, luxuriant undergrowth, tall, coarse grass, and vines, twisting and winding their long, serpentine folds around the trunks of the trees like huge, loathsome water-snakes. By the watch, we passed a mile-stone every three minutes and a half; and in less than nineteen minutes, arrived at the lake. Here, quite a village of handsome, white-painted hotels, cafés, dwellings, store-houses, and bathing rooms, burst at once upon our view; running past them, we gradually lessened our speed, and finally came to a full stop on the pier, where the rail-road terminates. Here we left the cars, which came thumping against each other successively, as they stopped; but the points of contact being padded, prevented any very violent shock to the occupants. The pier, constructed of piles and firmly planked over, was lined with sloops and schooners, which were taking in and discharging cargo, giving quite a bustling, business-like air to this infant port. Boys, ragged negroes, and gentlemen amateurs, were fishing in great numbers farther out in the lake; others were engaged in the delicate amusement of cray-fishing, while on the right the water was alive with bathers, who, disdaining the confined limits enclosed by the long white bathing-houses, which stretched along the south side of the pier, and yielding to the promptings of a watery ambition, were boldly striking out into the sluggish depths. To the east, the waters of the lake and sky met, presenting an ocean horizon to the untravelled citizens, who can have no other conception of the reality without taking a trip to the Balize. Light craft were skimming its waveless surface, under the influence of a gentle breeze, in all directions. A steamer, bearing the United States mail from Mobile, was seen in the distance, rolling out clouds of black smoke, and ploughing and dashing on her rapid way to the pier.

Retracing our steps to the head of the pier, we entered a very handsome *café*, or hotel, crowded with men. The eternal dominos were rattling on every table, glasses were ringing against glasses, and voices were heard, in high-toned conversation, in all languages, with mingled oaths and laughter; the noise and confusion were sufficient, without a miracle, to make a deaf man hear. All these persons, probably, were from the city, and had come down to the lake to amuse themselves, or kill an hour. The opposite *café* was equally crowded; while the billiard-rooms adjoining were filled with spectators and players. Clouds of tobacco-smoke enveloped the multitude, and the rooms rung with "Sacré bleu!" "Mon Dieu!" "Diable!" and blunt English oaths of equal force and import.

The first bell for the return had rung, and the passengers rushed to the cars, which were soon filled; the signal for starting was given, and the locomotive again led the van, with as much apparent importance as that with which the redoubtable and twice immortal Major Downing might be supposed to precede his gallant "rigiment of down easters." We had passed two-thirds of the distance when we were alarmed by a sudden and tremendous shouting from the forward car. The cry was echoed involuntarily along the whole train, and every head was instantly darted from the windows. The cause of the alarm was instantly perceptible. Less than a quarter of a mile ahead, a cow was lying very quietly and composedly, directly in the track of the flying cars. The shouts of the frightened passengers on discovering her, either petrified her with utter fear—for such yellings and whoopings were never heard before on this side Hades—or did not reach her, for she kept her position with the most complacent *nonchalance*. The engineer instantly stopped the locomotive, but though our momentum was diminished, it was too late to effect his object; in thirty seconds from the first discovery of the cow, the engine passed over the now terrified animal, with a jump—jump—and a grinding crash, and with so violent a shock as nearly to throw the car from the track; the next, and the next car followed—and the poor animal, the next instant, was left far behind, so completely severed, that the rear cars passed over her without any perceptible shock.

In a few minutes afterward, we arrived at the city, having been one minute longer in returning than in going to the lake. The rail-way has become, if not a very fashionable, at least a very general resort, for a great portion of the inhabitants of New-Orleans, particularly on Sabbaths and holydays. Lake Pontchartrain, the destination of all who visit the rail road for an excursion of pleasure, is, to New-Orleans, what Gray's Ferry was in the olden time to the good citizens of Philadelphia; or Jamaica pond is, at present, to the most worthy citizens of the emporium of notions; or what "Broad's" is to the gay citizens of Portland.[7] When we alighted from the car, the omnibus was at its stand at the head of the rail-way; so, jumping into it, with twenty others, the horn was blown with an emphasis, the whip was cracked with a series of inimitable flourishes, and in fifteen minutes after leaving the car, we were safely deposited near our hotel. If our jolting ride home, through the rough, deep-guttered streets, did not increase our appetite for the good things awaiting us at the *table d'hote,* it at least demonstrated to us the superiority of rail-ways over unpaved streets, which every now and then are intersected, for the sake of variety, with a gutter of no particular width, and a foot and a half deep, more or less, by the "lead."

FOOTNOTE

[7] The following sketch of the scenery and resources of Lake Pontchartrain is extracted from one of the New-Orleans papers, and is valuable for its general observations, and the correctness of its description of this theatre of summer amusement for the pleasure-seeking Orleanese:—

"Seven years ago there was but one steamboat plying the lakes in the vicinity of New-Orleans. There are now nine constantly departing from, and arriving at, the foot of the rail-road. They are generally crowded with passengers going to, and returning from the numerous villages which have sprung up in the woods that skirt the shores of Lake Borgne and Lake Pontchartrain, happy in the enjoyment of such facilities of escape from the heat and insalubrity of the city, and the anxious cares of business.

"This is the season for relaxation everywhere. It is, and should be, especially in New-Orleans, where the business of a year, by circumstances, is forced to be crowded into a few months, and where the people, during the season of business, are distinguished beyond any other for a devoted and untiring application to their affairs. If we may not here set apart a little time, and a little money, for amusement in summer, we know not where a claim for recreation and refreshment may be put forth. The fare on board the steam packets is extremely moderate, the accommodations good and convenient, the passages very agreeable, and the accommodations at the various public houses which line the shores, though not equalling the luxury and sumptuousness of the city houses, are sufficient for health and comfort. The moderate sums demanded from the passengers, and low price of board at the houses, enable young men to spend a month of leisure, at little, if any more cost, than the expenses of a month's residence in the city. The treat which they provide, in fish, fresh from the water, and in oysters from their banks, more than compensates for any difference in the meats of the market. Among the best houses on the borders of the lakes, are those, we believe, at Madisonville and Pascagoula, the first the nearest to, and the latter the farthest from the city; but in beauty of situation and scenery, all other spots are surpassed by that of the village at the bay of Beloxi, where, as yet, no house of public accommodation has been established. The curve of the bay is the line of beauty, the waves of old Ocean wash its margin, and his refreshing and invigorating airs whistle through the woods. There is a quiet and repose in the scene, not witnessed anywhere else along the voyage across the lakes. The neat, but scattering cottages lie seemingly imbedded among the rich and dark foliage of the back ground, and you fancy the inhabitants may be taking a Rip Van Winkle nap, of twenty years, a nap filled with dreams of the sweetest and most agreeable nature. We understand that there is yet land, fronting on the bay, which may be entered at the minimum price affixed by the government. In addition to the poetical attractions of the bay of Beloxi, we might add the substantial ones of—milk in abundance at a bit a quart—fish and wild fowl, (the latter just beginning to appear) plenty and cheap—and oysters at a bit a hundred.

"We are informed that the citizens of Mobile contemplate the erection of a splendid hotel on Dauphin Island, at the entrance of Mobile bay, immediately by which the steamboats pass on their way between Mobile bay and New-Orleans; and as the Mobilians seldom seriously contemplate any thing without carrying it into execution, we expect that in another year a common ground will be furnished, where the citizens of the two cities of the south-west may meet for their common amusement. The situation is healthful and agreeable, and we *hope,* as well as expect, that the project will be consummated."

XVII

During my accustomed peregrinations around the city yesterday, I dropped into the hall of the legislature, which was in session in the government house,—that large, handsome edifice, erected on Canal-street, alluded to in a former letter. The senate and house of representatives were literally *both* upper houses, being convened on the second floor of the building.

The rooms are large and sufficiently comfortable, though devoid of any architectural display. The number of senators is seventeen; of representatives, fifty. The majority, in both houses, are Creoles: there being, as I was informed, nine, out of the seventeen senators, French, and a small French majority in the house. The residue are *citizenized* northerners, and individuals from other states, who embody no mean portion of the political talents and statesman-like qualities of the legislature. Among many, to whom I had the pleasure of an introduction, and whose public characters are well and honourably known, I will mention Mr. Tenney, a native of New-Hampshire, and an alumnus of Dartmouth college. He has, like many other able and enterprising sons of New-England, struggled with no little distinction through all the vicissitudes of a young lawyer's career, till the suffrages of his adopted fellow-citizens have elevated him to the honourable station of senator, in the legislature of the state which he has chosen for his home. There are other northerners also, who, though in different stations, have arrived at distinction here. Their catalogue is not large, but it is brilliant with genius. The honourable career of the accomplished and lamented Gurley is well known to you. He was a man eminently distinguished, both for his public and social virtues; and in his death his adopted state has lost one of the brightest stars of her political constellation. And Ripley too, though shining in a southern sky, sheds a distinguished lustre over the "land of the north"—the country of his birth.

There is generally a large amount of business brought before this legislature, and its sessions seldom terminate before March or April. In their transactions, as a legislative body, there is a total absence of those little, though natural prejudices, which might be presumed to exist among members, so different from each other in education, language, and peculiarity of thought. If a bill is introduced by an American, the French members do not feel a disposition to oppose its passage on that account; nor, when it is brought in by a Frenchman, do they support it more eagerly or unanimously for that reason. A spirit of mutual cordiality, as great as can be looked for in a political assembly, pervades their whole body, to the entire exclusion of local prejudices. Neither is there an exclusive language used in their legislative proceedings. It is not necessary that the American members should speak French, or *vice versa*, though it would be certainly more agreeable were it universally understood by them; as all speeches made by Frenchmen, are immediately translated into English, while those made by the Americans are repeated again, by the translator, to the French part of the house, in their own language. This method not only necessarily consumes a great deal of time, and becomes excessively tedious to all parties, but diminishes, as do all translations, the strength, eloquence, and force of a speech; and, of course, lessens the impression. It is not a little amusing, to study the whimsical contortions of a Frenchman, while, with shrugging shoulders and restless eyes, he listens to, and watches the countenance of, some American party opponent, who may have the floor. The latter thunders out his torrent of eloquence, wherein the nicest epithets are not, perhaps, the most carefully chosen, in his zeal to express his political gall against his Gallic opponent; while monsieur fidgets about in happy ignorance, till the honourable member concludes,—when he jumps up, runs his open hand, chin, and nose, almost in the face of the interpreter, "*arrectis auribus*," and chafing like a lion; and before the last sentence is hurriedly completed, flings down his gantlet,—throws his whole soul into a rush of warm eloquence, beneath the edifying sound of which, his American antagonist feels that it is now his time to look foolish, which he does with a most commendable expression of mock *sang froid*, upon his twitching, try-to-be philosophic features.

The president of the senate and speaker of the house are Frenchmen: it is expected, however, that gentlemen filling these stations will readily speak French and English. By an act of a former legislature, slaves from other states could not be sold in this state, nor even those belonging to Louisiana, unless they were owned here previous to the passage of the law. The penalties for a violation of this law were fine and imprisonment to the vender, and the forfeiture of the slave, or his value. The law occasioned greater inconvenience to the citizens of the state, than its framers had foreseen. It again became a subject-matter for legislation, and a large portion of the members advocated its repeal. This was the subject of discussion when I was present, and the question of repeal was ably and warmly supported by Mr. Tenney, who is one of the state senators. Though he is doubtful whether the repeal will be effected this session, he is sanguine that it will be carried during the next annual assembly of the legislature.[8]

Leaving the government house, with its assembled wisdom, I repaired to my hotel, where I was to await the arrival of a friend, who had invited me to accompany him in a ride a few miles below the city on the banks of the river. I believe, in all my letters, I have yet been silent respecting this hotel; I will, however, while waiting for my equestrian friend, remedy that deficiency; for true to your wish, I will write of all and every thing worthy of notice; and I am half of your mind, that whatever is worthy the attention of a tourist, merits the passing record of his pen. "Bishop's hotel," so designated from its landlord, has been recently constructed, and is one of the largest in the Union. The Tremont possesses more architectural elegance; and Barnum's, the pride of Baltimore, is a handsomer structure. In the appearance of Bishop's, there is nothing imposing, but its height. It has two fronts, one on Camp, the other on Common-street. It is uniformly, with the exception of an angular tower, five stories in height; its bar-room is more than one hundred feet in length, and universally allowed to be the most splendid in America. The dining room, immediately over it, on the second floor, is of the same size; in which from two hundred and fifty to three hundred dine daily, of whom, probably, not twenty are French. The table is burthened with every luxury which can be procured in this luxurious climate. The servants are numerous, and with but two or three exceptions, slaves. They are willing, active, and intelligent. In this important point, Bishop's hotel is every way superior to the Tremont. There "pampered menials," whose every look and manner speak as plainly as anything but the tongue can speak, "if you desire anything of us, sir, be mighty civil, or you may whistle for it, for be assured, sir, that *we* are every whit as good as *you*." The insolence of these servants is already proverbial. But white servants, any where, and under any circumstances, are far from agreeable. In this point, and it is by no means an unimportant one, Bishop's is unequivocally superior to the Boston palace. With the coloured servant it is in verity, "Go, and he goeth—Come, and he cometh—Do this, and he doeth it."

The sleeping apartments are elegantly furnished, and carpeted, and well ventilated. There are two spacious drawing-rooms, contiguous to the magnificent dining hall, where lounging gentlemen can feel quite at home; and one of these contains a piano for the musical. From the top of the tower, which is one of the most elevated stations in the city, there is, to repay the fatigue of climbing the "weary, winding way," to the summit—a fine panoramic view of the whole city, with its sombre towers, flat roofs, long, dark, narrow streets, distant marshes, and the majestic Mississippi, sweeping proudly away to the north, and to the south, alive with dashing steamers, and glancing with white sails. The horizon, on every side, presents the same low, level, unrelieved line, that for ever meets the eye, which way soever it turns in the lower regions of the Mississippi. A day or two after I arrived here, I ascended to the top of this tower. The morning was brilliant, and the atmosphere was so pure, that distant objects seemed to be viewed through the purest crystalline medium. I would recommend every stranger, on his arrival at New-Orleans, to receive his first general impression of the city, from this eminence. He will regret, however, equally with others, that the pleasure he derives from the prospect cannot be enhanced by the aid of a good telescope, or even a common ship's spy-glass in either of which articles, the "lookout" is singularly deficient; but the enterprise, good taste, and obliging manner of Mr. Bishop have contributed in all else, throughout his extensive establishment, to the comfort, content, and amusement, of his numerous guests. A peculiarity in this hotel, and in one or two others here, is the exclusion of ladies from among the number of boarders; it is, properly, a bachelor establishment. There are, however, hotels of high rank in the city, where ladies and families are accommodated. They are kept by ladies, and often agreeably unite, with the public character of a hotel, the pleasures and advantages of social society. The boarding-house of Madame Wilkinson, widow of the late Gen. Wilkinson, a lady distinguished for her talents and accomplishments; that of Madame Herries, the widow of a titled foreigner, I believe, in Canal-street, and one or two others kept in good style, in Chartres-street, are the principal in the city.

Richardson's, a large hotel on Conti-street, is a bachelor establishment, where the up-country merchants usually put up, when they arrive in the city to purchase goods; though many of them, from choice or economy, remain as boarders or lodgers on board the steamers which bring them to New-Orleans, and on which, with their goods, they return to their homes. Young unmarried men here, usually have single furnished rooms, where they lodge, breakfast, and sup, dining at some hotel. There are, in some of the streets, long blocks of one story houses, with but one or two rooms in each, built purposely to be let out to bachelors. Indeed, there are neither hotels nor boarding-houses enough to accommodate one-tenth part of this class of forlorn bipeds. This independent way of living, in practice among so large a portion of the citizens and sojourners, in this city of anomalies, necessarily produces a peculiarity of character and habits among its observers, which has its natural and deteriorating effect upon the general state of society.

FOOTNOTE

[8] The law has recently been repealed.

XVIII

I intended in my last letter, to give you some account of an equestrian excursion along the banks of the river, and of a visit to the new Ursuline convent, two miles below the city; but a long digression about hotels and bachelors brought me to the end of my letter before I could even mention the subject. I will now fulfil my intention, in this letter, which will probably be the last you will receive from me, dated at New-Orleans.

Mounting our horses, at the door of the hotel, which were accoutred with clinking curbs, flashing martingales, and high-pummelled Spanish saddles, covered with blue broadcloth, the covering and housings being of one piece, as is the fashion here, we proceeded by a circuitous route to avoid the crowded front streets, toward the lower faubourg. In our ride, we passed the banks of the city, most of which are in Bienville-street or its vicinity. With but one exception, there is nothing in their external appearance to distinguish them from the other ordinary buildings, by which they are surrounded. The one referred to, whose denomination I do not recollect, is decidedly one of the handsomest structures in the south. It is lofty and extensive, with an imposing front and handsome columns, and stuccoed, so as to resemble the finest granite. And so perfect is the resemblance, that one can only assure himself that it is a deception, by reflecting that this beautiful material is used here little except in ornamental work; it being imported in small quantities from a great distance, by water, and its transportation being attended with too much expense to admit of its general adoption, as a material for building. The episcopal and presbyterian churches we also passed; both are plain buildings. Under the latter, an infant school is kept, which has been but lately organized, and is already very flourishing. It is under the care of northerners, as are most schools in this place, which are not French.

Of the permanent population of this city—which does not exceed fifty-one or two thousand, of whom thirty thousand are coloured—between fifteen and sixteen thousand are Catholics, and nearly six thousand Protestants; among whom are about seven hundred communicants. The

Catholic communicants number about six thousand and five hundred. There are ten Protestant churches, over which preside but seven or eight clergymen. Though the number of the former so much exceeds that of the latter, there are in this city in all, but six churches and chapels of the Catholic denomination, in which about twenty-five priests regularly officiate. There is here but one church to every three thousand and two hundred inhabitants, the estimate, for the most religious nations, being a church and clergyman for about every one thousand of the population.

As we rode along, I was struck with the appearance of the peculiar dress worn by the French inhabitants. The gentlemen, almost without exception, wear pantaloons of blue cottonade, coarse and unsightly in its appearance, but which many exquisites have recently taken a fancy to adopt. Their coats are seldom well fashioned; narrow, low collars, large flat buttons, hardly within hail of each other, and long, narrow skirts being the *bon-ton*. Their hats are all oddly shaped, and between the extremity of their pantaloons and their ill-shaped shoes, half a yard of blue striped yarn stocking shocks the fastidious eye. The ladies dress with taste, but it is French taste; with too much of the gew-gaw to please the plain republican, and, "by the same token," correct taste of a northerner. Many fine women, with brunette complexions, are to be seen walking the streets with the air of donnas. They wear no bonnets, but as a substitute, fasten a veil to the head; which, as they move, floats gracefully around them. These are termed "quadroons," one quarter of their blood being tinged with African. I have heard it remarked, that some of the finest looking women in New-Orleans are "quadroons." I know not how true this may be, but they certainly have large fine eyes, good features, magnificent forms, and elegantly shaped feet.

If a stranger should feel disposed to judge, whether the British watch-word, "Beauty and Booty," was based on a sufficient consideration, let him promenade the streets at twilight, and he will be convinced of the propriety of its first item. Then, windows, balconies, and doors, are alive with bright eyes, glancing scarfs, gay, bonnetless girls, playing children, and happy groups of every age. Street after street, square after square, will still present to him the same delightful scene of happy faces, and merry voices. The whole fair population seem to have abandoned their houses for the open air. How the bachelors of New-Orleans thread their way at sunset, through these brilliant groups of dark, sparkling eyes, without being burned to a cinder, passeth my comprehension. Every Sunday evening there is an extra turn out, when the whole city may be found promenading the noble Levée. This is an opportunity, which no stranger should omit, to observe the citizens under a new aspect. A ramble through the various streets, a few twilights successively, and a promenade on the Levée, on a Sabbath evening, will bring all the fair Creoles of the city, in review before him, and if that will not repay him for his trouble, let him go play "dominos!"

In our ride, we passed the commercial library. Its collection is valuable but not large. By the politeness of Monsieur D. I received a card for admittance during my stay; and I have found it an agreeable *oasis* of rest, after rambling for hours about the city. Its advantages in a place like this, where there are no circulating libraries, are very great. Passing the rail-way, in the vicinity of which is the Gentilly road, the famous duelling ground, we arrived at the "cotton press," a short distance below, on the left, fronting the river. It is a very extensive brick building with wings, having a yard in the rear, capable of containing fifty thousand bales of cotton. There is a rail-way, extending from the river to the press, on which the cotton is conveyed from the steamers, passing under a lofty arched way through the centre of the building, to the yard. All the cotton brought down the river, in addition to its original compression by hand, as it is baled up on the plantations, is again compressed by steam here, which diminishes the bale cubically, nearly one third. A ship can consequently take many more bales, than if the cotton were not thus compressed. There are, also, one or two more steam cotton-presses in the upper part of the city, which I have not had an opportunity of visiting. After passing this last building we overtook a cart loaded with negroes, proceeding to the country. To our inquiry, one of them answered,—while the others exhibited ivory enough to sheathe a ship's bottom, "We Wirginny niggurs, Massas: new massa, he juss buy us, and we be gwine to he plantation. Plenty sugar dere, massa!" They all appeared contented and happy, and highly elated at their sweet anticipations. Say not that the slavery of the Louisiana negroes is a *bitter* draught.

An old, plain, unassuming, and apparently deserted building, a little retired from the road and half-hidden in shrubbery, next attracted our attention. Over its front was a sign informing us that it was the "Lyceum pour les jeunes gens." We could not learn whether it had teacher or pupil, but from appearances we inferred that it was minus both. A padre, in the awkward black gown peculiar to his order, which is seldom laid aside out of doors, passed just at this time; and to our inquiries respecting the lyceum, though framed, *me judice*, in very respectable *lingua Franca*, he deigned us no other reply than a pleasant smile, and a low-toned, sonorous "Benedicite."

With others, we were equally unsuccessful. One, of whom we inquired, and who appeared as though he might find an amber-stone among a heap of pebbles, if he were previously informed that it was the colour of whiskey—replied, "Why, I dont cozactly know, stranngers, seeing I aint used to readin', overmuch, but to my eye, it looks consarnedly like a tavern-sign."

"Why do you think so, my man?"

"Why, you see, I can't, somehow, make out the first part; but the last word spells gin, as slick as a tallow whistle—I say, strannger, ye haint got nothin o' no small-sized piccaiune about ye, have ye?"—We threw our intelligent informant, who was no doubt some stray prodigal son from old Kentuck or down east—though his ignorance of the art of reading belied his country—the required fee for his information, and continued our ride. We were now quite out of the city; the noble Mississippi rolled proudly toward the sea on our right, its banks unrelieved by a single vessel:—while on our left, embowered in shrubbery, public and private buildings lined the road, which wound pleasantly along the level borders of the river.

Shortly after leaving the Lyceum, we noticed on our left, at some distance from the road, a large building, of more respectable appearance and dimensions than the last. A sign here too informed us, whatever our ingenious literary sign-reader might have rendered it, that *there* was the "College Washington." Our information respecting this institution was in every respect as satisfactory as that which we had obtained concerning the Lyceum. Not an individual urchin, or grave instructer, was to be seen at the windows, or within the precincts. Its halls were silent and deserted. I have made inquiries, since I returned, of old residents, respecting it. No one knows any thing of it. Some may have heard there was such a college. Some may even have seen the sign, in passing: but the majority learned for the first time, from my inquiries, that there was such an institution in existence. So we are all equally wise respecting it. Passing beautiful cottages, partially hidden in foliage, tasteful villas, and deserted mansions, alternately, our attention was attracted by a pretty residence, far from the road, at the extremity of an extensive grass-plat, void of shrub or any token of horticultural taste. Had the grounds been ornamented, like all others in the vicinity, with shrubbery, it would have been one of the loveliest residences on the road; but, as it was, its aspect was dreary. We were informed that it was the residence of the British consul; but he seems to have left his national passion for ornamental gardening, shrubbery walks, and park-like grounds, at home; denying himself their luxurious shade and agreeable beauty, in a climate where, alone, they are really necessary for comfort—where the cool covert of a thickly foliaged tree is as great a luxury to a northerner, as a welling fountain in the desert to the fainting Arab.

In a short ride from the residence of the consul, we arrived opposite to the Ursuline convent, a very large and handsome two-story edifice, with a high Spanish roof, heavy cornices, deep windows, half concealed by the foliage of orange and lemon trees, and stuccoed, in imitation of rough white marble. Three other buildings, of the same size, extended at the rear of this main building, forming three sides of the court of the convent, of which area this formed the fourth, each building fronting within upon the court, as well as without. There are about seventy young ladies pursuing a course of education here—some as boarders, and others as day scholars. The boarders are kept very rigidly. They are permitted to leave the convent, to visit friends in the city, if by permission of parents, but once a month. None are allowed to see them, unless they first obtain written permission, from the parents or guardians of the young ladies.

As my friend had an errand at the convent, we called. Proceeding down a long avenue to the portal on the right side of the grounds, we entered, and applied our riding whips to the door for admission. We were questioned by an unseen querist, as to our business there, as are all visiters. The voice issued from a tin plate, perforated with innumerable little holes, and resembling a colander fixed in the wall, on one side of the entrance. If the visiters give a good account of themselves, and can show good cause why they should speak with any of the young ladies, they are told to open the door at the left; whereupon, they find themselves in a long, dimly-lighted apartment, without any article of furniture, except a backless form. Three sides of this room are like any other—but, the fourth is open to the inner court, and latticed from the ceiling to the floor, like a summer-house. Approaching the lattice, the visiter, by placing his eye to the apertures, has a full view of the interior, and the three inner fronts of the convent. A double cloister extends above and below, and around the whole court; where the young ladies may be seen walking, studying, or amusing themselves. She, for whom the visiter has inquired, now approaches the grate demurely by the side of one of the elderly ladies of the sisterhood; and the visiter, placing his lips to an aperture, as to the mouth of a speaking trumpet, must address her, and thus carry on his conversation; while the elder nun stands within earshot, that peradventure she may thereby be edified.

The young ladies are here well and thoroughly educated;—even dancing is not prohibited, and is taught by a professor from the city. The religious exercises of the convent are of course Roman Catholic; but no farther than the daily routine of formal religious services, are the tenets of their faith inculcated upon the minds of the pupils. Some Protestant young ladies, allured by the romantic and imposing character of the Catholic religion, embrace it: but a few years after leaving the convent, are generally sufficient to efface their new faith and bring them back to the religion of their childhood. But the instances are very rare in which a Protestant becomes a *religieuse,* or leaves the convent a Catholic: though a great portion of the young ladies under the charge of the Ursuline sisterhood are of Protestant parentage.

The remainder of our ride was past orange gardens and French villas, so like all we had passed nearer the city, that they presented no variety; after riding a mile below the convent, we turned our horses' heads back to the city, and in less than an hour arrived at our hotel just in time to sit down to one of Bishop's sumptuous dinners.

XIX

I have just returned from a visit to the scene of American resolution and individual renown—the battle-ground of New-Orleans. The Aceldama, where one warrior-chief drove his triumphal car over the grave of another—the field of "fame and of glory" from which the "hero of two wars" plucked the chaplet which encircles his brow, and the *éclat* which has elevated him to a throne!—

The field of battle lies between five and six miles below the city, on the left bank, on the New-Orleans side of the river. The road conducting us to it, wound pleasantly along the Levée; its unvarying level relieved by delightful gardens, and pleasant country seats—(one of which, constructed like a Chinese villa, struck me as eminently tasteful and picturesque)—skirting it upon one side, and by the noble, lake-like Mississippi on the other, which, beating upon its waveless bosom a hundred white sails, and a solitary tow-boat leading, like a conqueror, a fleet in her train—rolled silently and majestically past to the ocean. When, in our own estimation, and, no doubt, in that of our horses, we had accomplished the prescribed two leagues, we reined up at a steam saw-mill, erected and in full operation on the road-side, and inquired for some directions to the spot—not discerning in the peaceful plantations before us, any indications of the scene of so fierce a struggle as that which took place, when England and America met in proud array, and the military standards of each gallantly waved to the "battle and the breeze." Although, on ascending the river in the ship, I obtained a moonlight glance of the spot, I received no impression of its *locale* sufficiently accurate to enable me to recognise it under different circumstances. An extensive, level field was spread out before us, apparently the peaceful domain of some planter, who probably resided in a little piazza-girted cottage which stood on the banks of the river. But this field, we at once decided, could not be the battle-field—so quiet and farm-like it reposed. "There," was our reflection, "armies can never have met! there, warriors can never have stalked in the pride of victory with

"— — garments rolled in blood!"

Yet peaceful as it slumbered there, that domain had once rung with the clangor of war. It *was* the battle-field! But silence now reigned

"— — where the free blood gushed
When England came arrayed—
So many a voice had there been hushed;
So many a footstep stayed."

In reply to our inquiries, made of one apparently superintending the steam-works, we received simply the tacit "Follow me gentlemen!" We gladly accommodated the paces of our spirited horses to those of our obliging and very practical informant, who alertly preceded us, blessing the stars which had given us so unexpectedly a cicerone, who, from his vicinity to the spot must be *au fait* in all the interesting minutiæ of so celebrated a place. Following our guide a few hundred yards farther down the river-road, we passed on the left hand a one story wooden dwelling-house situated at a short distance back from the road, having a gallery, or portico in front, and elevated upon a basement story of brick, like most other houses built immediately on the river. This, our guide informed us, was "the house occupied by General Jackson as head-quarters: and there," he continued, pointing to a planter's residence two or three miles farther down the river, "is the mansion-house of General, (late governor, Villeré) which was occupied by Sir Edward Packenham as the head-quarters of the British army."

"But the battle-ground—where is that sir?" we inquired, as he silently continued his rapid walk in advance of us.

"There it is," he replied after walking on a minute or two longer in silence, and turning the corner of a narrow, fenced lane which extended from the river to the forest-covered marshes—"there it is, gentlemen,"—and at the same time extended his arm in the direction of the peaceful plain, which we had before observed,—spread out like a carpet, it was so very level—till it terminated in the distant forests, by which and the river it was nearly enclosed. Riding a quarter of a mile down the lane we dismounted, and leaving our horses in the road, sprang over a fence, and in a few seconds stood upon the American breast-works!

"When," said a mercurial friend lately, in describing his feelings on first standing upon the same spot—"when I leaped upon the embankment, my first impulse was to give vent to my excited feelings by a shout that might have awakened the mailed sleepers from their sleep of death." Our emotions—for strong and strange emotions will be irresistibly excited in the breast of every one, "to war's dark scenes unused," on first beholding the scene of a sanguinary conflict, between man and man, whether it be grisly with carnage, pleasantly waving with the yellow harvest, or carpeted with green—our emotions, though perhaps equally deep, exhibited themselves very differently. For some moments, after gaining our position, we stood wrapped in silence. The wild and terrible scenes of which the ground we trod had been the theatre, passed vividly before my mind with almost the distinctness of reality, impressing it with reflections of a deep and solemn character. I stood upon the graves of the fallen! Every footfall disturbed human ashes! Human dust gathered upon our shoes as the dust of the plain! My thoughts were too full for utterance. "On the very spot where I stand"—thought I, "some gallant fellow poured out the best blood of his heart! Here, past me, and around me, flowed the sanguinary tide of death!—The fierce battle-cry—the bray of trumpets—the ringing of steel on steel—the roar of artillery hurling leaden and iron hail against human breasts—the rattling of musketry—the shouts of the victor, and the groans of the wounded, were here mingled—a whirlwind of noise and death!"

"Under those two oaks, which you see about half a mile over the field, Sir Edward was borne, by his retreating soldiers, to die"—said our guide, suddenly interrupting my momentary reverie. I looked in the direction indicated by his finger, and my eyes rested upon a venerable oak, towering in solitary grandeur over the field, and overshadowing the graves of the slain, who, in great numbers, had been sepultured beneath its shadow. How many eyes were fixed, with the fond recollection of their village homes amid clustering oaks in distant England, upon this noble tree—which, in a few moments, amid the howl of war, were closed for ever in the sleep of the dead! Of how many last looks were its branches the repositories! How many manly sighs were wafted toward its waving summit from the breast of many a brave man, who was never more to behold the wave of a green tree upon the pleasant earth!

It has been stated that Sir Edward Packenham fell, and was buried under this oak, or these oaks, (for I believe there are two,) but I have been informed, since my return from the field, by a gentleman who was commander of a troop of horse in the action, that when the British retreated, he saw from the parapet the body of General Packenham lying alone upon the ground, surrounded by the dead and wounded, readily distinguishable by its uniform; and, that during the armistice for the burial of the dead, he saw his body borne from the field by the British soldiers, who afterward conveyed it with them in their retreat to their fleet.

The rampart of earth upon which we stood, presented very little the appearance of having ever been a defence for three thousand breasts; resembling rather one of the numerous dikes constructed on the plantations near the river, to drain the very marshy soil which abounds in this region, than the military defences of a field of battle. It was a grassy embankment, extending, with the exception of an angle near the forest—about a mile in a straight line from the river to the cypress swamps in the rear; four feet high, and five or six feet broad. At the time of the battle it was the height of a man, and somewhat broader than at present, and along the whole front ran a *fossé,* containing five feet of water, and of the same breadth as the parapet. This was now nearly filled with earth, and could easily be leaped over at any point. The embankment throughout the whole extent is much worn, indented and, occasionally, levelled with the surface of the plain. Upon the top of it, before the battle, eight batteries were erected, with embrasures of cotton bales, piled transversely. Under cover of this friendly embankment, the Americans lay *perdus,* but not idle, during the greater portion of the battle.

A daring Tennessean, with a blanket tied round him, and a hat with a brim of enormous breadth, who seemed to be fighting "on his own hook," disdaining to raise his rifle over the bank of earth and fire, in safety to his person, like his more wary fellow soldiers, chose to spring, every time he fired, upon the breastwork, where, balancing himself, he would bring his rifle to his cheek, throw back his broad brim, take sight and fire, while the enemy were advancing to the attack, as deliberately as though shooting at a herd of deer; then leaping down on the inner side, he would reload, mount the works, cock his beaver, take aim, and crack again. "This he did," said an English officer, who was taken prisoner by him, and who laughingly related it as a good anecdote to Captain D— —, my informant above alluded to—"five times in rapid succession, as I advanced at the head of my company, and though the grape whistled through the air over our heads, for the life of me I could not help smiling at his grotesque demi-savage, demi-quaker figure, as he threw back the broad flap of his castor to obtain a fair sight—deliberately raised his rifle—shut his left eye, and blazed away at us. I verily believe he brought down one of my men at every shot."

As the British resolutely advanced, though columns fell like the tall grain before the sickle at the fire of the Americans, this same officer approached at the head of his brave grenadiers amid the rolling fire of musketry from the lines of his unseen foes, undaunted and untouched. "Advance, my men!" he shouted as he reached the edge of the *fossé*—

"follow me!" and sword in hand he leaped the ditch, and turning amidst the roar and flame of a hundred muskets to encourage his men, beheld to his surprise but a single man of his company upon his feet—more than fifty brave fellows, whom he had so gallantly led on to the attack, had been shot down. As he was about to leap back from his dangerous situation, his sword was shivered in his grasp by a rifle ball, and at the same instant the daring Tennessean sprang upon the parapet and levelled his deadly weapon at his breast, calmly observing, "Surrender, strannger—or, I may perforate ye!" "Chagrined," said the officer, at the close of his recital, "I was compelled to deliver to the bold fellow my mutilated sword, and pass over into the American lines."

"Here," said our guide and cicerone, advancing a few paces up the embankment, and placing his foot emphatically upon the ground, "*here* fell Renie."

This gallant man, with the calf of his leg shot away by a cannon-ball, leaped upon the breast-works with a shout of exultation, and was immediately shot through the heart, by an American private. Packenham, the favourite *elêve* of Wellington, and the "beau ideal" of a British soldier, after receiving a second wound, while attempting to rally his broken columns, fell directly in front of our position, not far from where Renie received his death-wound. In the disorder and panic of the first retreat of the British, he was left bleeding and forsaken among the dead and dying. Not far from this melancholy spot, Gibbes received his mortal wound; and near the place where this gallant officer fell, one of the staff of the English general was also shot down. The whole field was fruitful with scenes of thrilling interest. I should weary you by individualizing them. There was scarcely a spot on which I could cast my eyes, where a soldier had not poured out his life-blood. "As I stood upon the breast-works," said Captain Dunbar, "after the action, the field of battle before me was so thickly strewn with dead bodies, that I could have walked fifty yards over them without placing my foot upon the ground." How revolting the sight of a field thus sown must be to human nature! Man must indeed be humbled at such a spectacle.

We walked slowly over the ground, which annually waves with undulating harvests of the rich cane. Our guide was intelligent and sufficiently communicative without being garrulous. He was familiar with every interesting fact associated with the spot, and by his correct information rendered our visit both more satisfactory and agreeable than it otherwise would have been.

"Here gentilhommes, j'ai findé some bullet for you to buy," shouted a little French mulatto at the top of his voice, who, among other boys of various hues, had followed us to the field, "me, j'ai trop— too much;" and on reaching us, this double-tongued urchin turned his pockets inside out and discharged upon the ground a load of rusty grape shot, bullets, and fragments of lead—his little stock in trade, some, if not all of which, I surmised, had been manufactured for the occasion.

"Did you find them on the battle-ground, garçon?"

"Iss—oui, Messieurs, me did, de long-temps."

I was about to charge him with having prepared his pockets before leaving home, when Mr. C. exhibited a grape shot that he had picked from the dark soil in which it was half buried. I bought for a piccaiune,[9] the smallest currency of the country, the "load of grape," and we pursued our walk over the field, listening with much interest to the communications of our guide, conjuring up the past scenes of strife and searching for balls; which by and by began to thicken upon us so fast, that we were disposed to attribute a generative principle to grape-shot. We were told by our cicerone that they were found in great numbers by the ploughmen, and disposed of to curious visiters. On inquiring of him if false ones were not imposed upon the unsuspecting, he replied "No—there is no need of that—there is an abundance of those which are genuine."

"I'm got half a peck on um to hum, mysef, I'se found," exclaimed a little negro in a voice that sounded like the creaking of a shoe, bolting off at the same time for the treasure, like one of his own cannon-balls. What appalling evidence is this abundance of leaden and iron hail strewed over the field, of the terrible character of that war-storm which swept so fearfully over it. Flattened and round balls, grape of various sizes, and non-descript bits of iron were the principal objects picked up in our stroll over the ground.

The night was rapidly approaching—for we had lingered long on this interesting spot—and precluded our visit to the oaks, to which it had been our intention to extend our walk; and as we turned to retrace our steps with our pockets heavy with metal, something rang to the touch of my foot, which, on lifting and cleansing it from the loam, we discovered to be the butt-piece of a musket. As this was the most valuable relic which the field afforded, C. was invested with it, for the purpose of placing it in the museum or Codman's amateur collection, for the benefit of the curious, when he returns to that land of curious bipeds, where such kind of mementos are duly estimated. Twilight had already commenced, as, advancing over the same ground across which the gallant Packenham led his veteran army, we fearlessly leaped the fossé and, unresisted, ascended the parapet. Hastening to free our impatient horses from their thraldom, we mounted them, and—not forgetting a suitable douceur, by way of "a consideration" to our obliging cicerone—spurred for the city. As we arrived at the head of the lane and emerged again upon the high-way, I paused for an instant upon the summit of the Levée to take a last view of the battle-ground which lay in calm repose under the gathering twilight—challenging the strongest exercise of the imagination to believe it ever to have borne other than its present rural character, or echoed to other sounds than the whistle of the careless slave as he cut the luxuriant cane, the gun of the sportsman, or the melancholy song of the plough-boy.

FOOTNOTE

[9] Properly, *piccaillon*, but pronounced as in the text. Called in New England a "four pence half penny," in New-York a "sixpence," and in Philadelphia a "fip."

XX

The spacious bar-room of our magnificent hotel, as I descended to it on Sabbath morning, resounded to the footsteps of a hundred gentlemen, some promenading and in earnest conversation—some hastening to, or lounging about the bar, that magnet of attraction to thirsty spirits, on which was displayed a row of rapidly disappearing glasses, containing the tempting, green-leaved, mint-julep—while, along the sides of the large room, or clustered around the tall, black columns, which extended through the centre of the hall, were others, some *tête à tête*, and others again smoking, and sipping in quiet their morning potation. A few, with legs *à la Trollope*, upon the tables, were reading stray papers, and at the farther extremity of the hall, standing around a lofty desk, were ranks of merchants similarly engaged. My northern friend, with whom I had planned a visit to the cathedral, met me at the door of the hotel, around which, upon the side-walk, was gathered a knot of fashionably dressed, cane-wearing young men, talking, all together, of a duel that had taken place, or was about to "come off," we could not ascertain exactly which, from the few words heard in passing to the street. This, by the by, is a frequent theme of conversation here, and too often based upon facts to be one of light moment.[10]

The morning was cloudless and beautiful. The air was mild, and for the city, elastic and exhilarating. The sun shone down warm and cheerfully, enlivening the spirits, and making all things glad with its brightness. The whole city had come forth into the streets to enjoy it; and as we passed from Camp-street across Canal, into Chartres-street, all the gay inhabitants, one would verily believe, had turned out as to a gala. The long, narrow streets were thronged with moving multitudes, and flashing with scarfs, ribbons, and feathers. Children, with large expressive eyes, and clustering locks, their heads surmounted with tasselled caps and fancy hats, arrayed in their "brightest and best," bounded along behind their more soberly arrayed, but not less gay parents, followed by gaudily dressed slaves, who chattered incessantly with half-suppressed laughter to their acquaintances on the opposite trottoir. Clerks, just such looking young men as you will meet on Sabbath mornings in Broadway, or Cornhill—released from their six days' confinement—lounged by us arm in arm, as fine as the tailor and hair-dresser could make them. Crowds, or gangs of American and English sailors, mingling most companionably, on a cruise through the city, rolled jollily along—the same careless independent fellows that they are all the world over. I have observed that in foreign ports, the seamen of these once hostile nations link together like brothers. This is as it should be. The good feeling existing generally among all classes of Americans toward the mother country, must be gratifying both to reflecting Americans and to Englishmen. These sons of Neptune were all dressed nearly alike in blue jackets, and full white trowsers, with black silk handkerchiefs knotted carelessly around their necks, and confined by some nautical breast-pin, in the shape of a foul anchor, a ship under her three top-sails, or plain gold hearts, pierced by arrows. Sailors are very sentimental fellows on shore! In direct contrast to these frank-looking, open-browed tars, who yawed along the side-walk, as a landsman would walk on a ship's deck at sea, we passed, near the head of Bienville-street, a straggling crew of some Spanish trader, clothed in tarry pantaloons and woollen shirts, and girt about with red and blue sashes, bucanier fashion, with filthy black whiskers, and stealthy glowing eyes, who glided warily along with lowering brows. The unsailor-like French sailor—the half horse and half alligator Kentucky boatman—the gentlemanly, carelessly-dressed cotton planter—the pale valetudinarian, from the north, whose deep sunken eye told of suicidal vigils over the midnight lamp—a noble looking foreigner, and a wretched beggar—a troop of Swiss emigrants, from the grand sire to the infant, and a gang of Erin's toil-worn exiles—all mingled *en masse*—swept along in this living current; while, gazing down upon the moving multitude from lofty balconies, were clusters of bright eyes, and sunny faces flashed from every window.

As we approached the cathedral, a dark-hued and finely moulded quadroon, with only a flowing veil upon her head, glided majestically past us. The elegant olive-browned Louisianese—the rosy-cheeked maiden from *La belle riviere*—the Parisian gentilhomme—a dignified, light-mustachoed palsgrave, and a portly sea-captain—the haughty Englishman and prouder southerner—a blanketed Choctaw, and a negro in uniform—slaves and freed-men of every shade, elbowed each other very familiarly as they traversed in various directions the crowded side-walks.

Crossing rue St. Louis, we came in collision with a party of gens d'armes with drawn swords in their hands, which they used as walking canes, leading an unlucky culprit to the calaboose—that "black-hole" of the city. Soldiers in splendid uniforms, with clashing and jingling accoutrements, were continually hurrying past us to parade. At the corner of Toulouse-street we met a straggling procession of bare-headed, sturdy-looking priests, in soiled black surplices and fashionable boots, preceded by half a dozen white-robed boys, bare-legged and dirty. By this dignified procession, among which the crowd promiscuously mingled as they passed along, and whose august approach is usually notified by the jingling of the "sacring bell," was borne the sacred "host." They hastily passed us, shoved and jostled by the crowd, who scarcely gave way to them as they hastened on their ghostly message. These things are done differently in Buenos Ayres or Rio Janeiro, where such a procession is escorted by an armed guard, and a bayonet thrust, or a night in a Spanish prison, is the penalty for neglecting to genuflect, or uncover the heretical head. As we issued from Chartres-street—where all "nations and kingdoms and tongues" seemed to have united to form its pageant of life—upon the esplanade in front of the cathedral, we were surprised by the sound of martial music pealing clearly above the confusion of tongues, the tramp of feet, and the rattling of carriages. On and around the noble green, soldiers in various uniforms, some of them of a gorgeous and splendid description, were assembling for parade. Members of the creole regiment—the finest body of military men I ever beheld, with the exception of a Brazilian regiment of blacks—were rapidly marshalling in the square. And mounted hussars, with lofty caps and in glittering mail, were thundering in from the various streets, their spurs, chains and sabres, ringing and jingling warlike music, as they dashed up to the rendezvous.

At the head of this noble square, so variegated and tumultuous with its dazzling mimicry of war, rose in solemn and imposing grandeur the venerable cathedral, lifting its heavy towers high above the emmet-crowd beneath. Its doors, in front of which was extended a line of carriages, were thronged with a motley crowd, whose attention was equally divided between the religious ceremonies within the temple and the military display without. We forced our way through the mass, which was composed of strangers like ourselves—casual spectators—servants—hack-drivers—fruit sellers, and some few, who, like the publican, worshipped "afar off."

It was the celebration of the Eucharist. Within, crowds were kneeling upon the pavement under the corridor and along the aisles—some in attitudes of the profoundest humility and awe. Others were kneeling, as nominal Protestants stand in prayer, without intention or feeling of humility; but merely assuming the posture as a matter of form. Among these last were many young Frenchmen, whose pantaloons were kept from soiling by white handkerchiefs as they kneeled, playing with their watch-guards, twirling their narrow-brimmed silk hats, or gazing idly about over the prostrate multitude. Here and there kneeled a fine female figure; and dark eyes from artfully arranged veils wandered every where but over the missal, clasped in unconscious fingers. At the base of a massive column two fair girls, kneeling side by side, were laughingly whispering together. But there were also venerable sires with locks of snow, and aged matrons, and manly forms of men, and graceful women, maidens and children, who bowed with their faces to the ground in deep devotion. As we entered, the solemn peal of an organ, mingled with the deep toned voices of the priests chanting the imposing mass, rolled over the prostrate assembly; at the same moment the host was elevated and the multitude, bowing their foreheads to the pavement, profoundly adored this Roman *schechinah*, or *visible* presence of the Saviour.

Having, with some difficulty, worked our way through the worshippers, who, after the solemn service of the consecration of the bread and wine was finished, arose from their knees, we gained an eligible situation by one of the pillars which support the vaulted roof, and there took our post of observation. A marble font of holy water stood near us on our right hand, into which all true Catholics who entered or departed from the church, dipped the tip of a finger, with the greatest possible veneration; and therewith—the while moving their lips with a brief, indistinctly-heard prayer—crossed themselves upon both the forehead and the breast. This ceremony was also performed by proxy. A very handsome French lady entered the church, while we leaned against the column, and advancing directly to the font, dipped her ungloved finger into the consecrated laver, made the sign of the cross first upon her own fine forehead, and then turning, stooped down and crossed affectionately and prayerfully the pure, olive brows of two beautiful little girls who followed her, and the forehead of an infant borne in the arms of a slave; who, dipping her tawny fingers in the water, blessed her own black forehead; and then all passed up the aisle toward the altar—a sanctified family! How like infant baptism, this beautiful and affecting little scene of a mother thus blessing in the sincerity of her heart, her innocent offspring! White, black, and yellow—the rich and the poor, the freeman and slave, all dipped in the same font—were all blessed by the same water. A beautiful emblem of the undistinguishing blood of the Saviour of the world!

Not far from this holy vessel, behind a table or temporary altar, sat a man with a scowling brow and a superstitious eye, coarsely dressed, without vest or cravat. Before him lay a large salver strewed in great profusion with pieces of silver coin from a *bit* to a dollar. On the centre, and only part of the waiter not piled with money, lay a silver crucifix. At the moment this display caught our eyes, and before we had time to form any conjectures as to its object, a mulatress gave us the desired explanation. Crossing from the broad aisle of the church, she reverently approached the spot and kneeling before the altar, added a quarter of a dollar to the glittering pile, and bending over, kissed first the feet, then the knees, hands, and wounded side of the image, while real tears flowed down her saffron cheeks. Elevating her prostrate form, she passed to the font, dipped her finger in the holy water and disappeared amid the crowd at the door. A gay demoiselle tripping lightly past us, bent on one knee before the waiter, threw down upon it a heavy piece of silver, and, less humble than the one who had preceded her, imprinted a kiss upon the metal lips of the image and glided from the cathedral. She was followed by a lame negro, darker than Othello, uglier and more clumsy than Caliban, who for a piccaiune, which tinkled upon the salver, had the privilege of saluting the senseless image from head to foot in the most devotional and lavish manner. A little child, led by its nurse, followed, and timidly, at the direction of its coloured governess, kissed the calm and expansive forehead of the sculptured idol. During the half hour we remained, there was a continual flow of the current of devotees to this spot, in their way to and from the high altar. But I observed that ten blacks approached the crucifix for every white!

This altar with its enriched salver is merely a Roman Catholic "contribution-box,"—a new way of doing an old thing. Some of the Protestant churches resound with a sacred hymn, or the voice of the clergyman reading a portion of the liturgy or discipline, calculated to inspire charitable feelings, while the contribution-box or bag makes its begging tour among the pews. In the cathedral the same feelings are excited by an appeal to the senses through the silent exhibition of the sufferings of the Redeemer. With one, the ear is the road to the heart, with the other, the eye; but if it is only reached, it were useless to quibble about the medium of application.

I lingered long after the great body of the congregation had departed. Here and there, before a favourite shrine—the tutelary guardian of the devotee—kneeled only a solitary individual. Close by my side, before the pictured representation of a martyrdom, bent a female form enveloped in mourning robes, her features concealed in the folds of a rich black veil. Far off, before the distant shrine of the Virgin Mother, knelt a very old man engaged in inaudible prayer, with his head pressed upon the cold stone pavement. Slowly and reflectingly I paced the deserted aisles toward the high altar, which stood in the midst of a splendid and dazzling creation of gold and silver, rich colouring, architectural finery, and gorgeous decorations, burning tapers, and candlesticks like silver pillars; the whole extending from the pavement to the ceiling, and all so mingled and confused in the religious gloom of the church, that I was unable to analyse or form any distinct idea of it. But the *coup d'œil* was unrivalled by any display I had ever seen in an American temple.

At the lower termination of the side aisles of the cathedral, stood dark mahogany confessionals, with blinds at the sides—reminding one of sentry boxes. These, however, were deserted and apparently seldom occupied. Sins must be diminished here, or penitents have grown more discreet than in former times! In a little while the cathedral, save by a poor woman kneeling devoutly before a wretched picture, which I took to be a representation of the martyrdom of saint Peter, became silent and deserted. While gazing upon the image of the Virgin Mary, arrayed like a prima donna, and profusely decorated with finery, standing pensively within an isolated niche, to the left of the grand altar, a slight noise, and the simultaneous agitation of a curtain, drew my attention to the entrance of a trio of young ladies, through a side door hitherto concealed behind the arras, preceded by an elderly brown-complexioned lady, of the most duenna-like physiognomy and bearing. Without noticing the presence of a stranger and a heretic—for I was gazing most undevoutly and heretically upon the jewelled image before me as they entered—they dipped the tips of their fingers in a font of holy water which stood by the entrance—passed into the centre aisle in front of the great crucifix, and kneeling in a cluster upon a rich carpet, spread upon the pavement over the crypts of the distinguished dead, by a female slave who attended them, were at once engaged in the most absorbing devotion. After a short period they arose—bowed sweepingly to the crucifix, genuflected most gracefully with a sort of familiar nod of recognition before the shrine of the Virgin, and moistening the ends of their fingers again in the marble basin, quietly disappeared.

I was now alone in the vast building. Though the current of human life flowed around its walls, with a great tumult of mingled sounds, yet only a noise, like the faintly heard murmuring of distant surf, penetrated its massive walls, and broke a silence like that of the grave which reigned within. The illustrious dead slept beneath the hollow pavement, which echoed to my footfall like a vaulted sepulchre. The ghastly images of slaughtered men looked down upon me from the walls, with agony depicted on their pale and unearthly countenances, seen indistinctly through the dim twilight of the place. The melancholy tapers burned faintly before the deserted shrines, increasing, rather than illuminating the gloom of the venerable temple. Gradually, under the combined influence of these gloomy objects, I felt a solemnity stealing over me, awed and depressed by the tomb-like repose that reigned around. Suddenly the clear light of noon-day flashed in through the drawn curtain, and another worshipper entered. Turning to take a last glance at the interior of this imposing fabric, so well calculated to excite the religious feelings of even a descendant of the Puritans, I drew aside the curtain, and the next moment was involved in the life, bustle, and tumult of the streets of a large city, whose noise, confusion, and bright sunshine contrasted strangely with the perfect stillness and "dim religious light" of the cathedral.

FOOTNOTE

[10] The rage for duelling is at such a pitch, that a jest or smart repartee is sufficient excuse for a challenge, in which powder and ball are the arguments. The Court of honour has proved unsuccessful in its operation, and no person, it is said, has yet dared to stem the current of popular opinion. The accuracy of the Creoles, with the pistol, is said to be astonishing, and no youngster springing into life, is considered entitled to the claims of manhood, until made the mark of an adversary's bullet. In their shooting galleries, the test of their aim is firing at a button at ten or twelve paces distance, suspended by a wire, which, when struck, touches a spring that discloses a flag. There are but few who miss more than once in three times. An appointment for a duel is talked of with the *nonchalance* of an invitation to a dinner or supper party.

XXI

229

"Do you attend the *Theatre d'Orleans* to night?" inquired a young Bostonian, forgetful of his orthodox habits—last Sabbath evening, twirling while he spoke a ticket in his fingers—"you know the maxim—when one is in Rome"—

"I have not been here quite long enough yet to apply the rule," said I; "is not the theatre open on other evenings of the week?" "Very seldom," he replied, "unless in the gayest part of the season—though I believe there is to be a performance some night this week; I will ascertain when and accompany you."

You are aware that the rituals, or established forms of the Roman church, do not prohibit amusements on this sacred day. The Sabbath, consequently, in a city, the majority of whose inhabitants are Catholics, is not observed as in the estimation of New-Englanders, or Protestants it should be. The lively Orleanese defend the custom of crowding their theatres, attending military parades, assembling in ball-rooms, and mingling in the dangerous masquerade on this day, by wielding the scriptural weapon—"the Sabbath was made for man—not man for the Sabbath;" and then making their own inductions, they argue that the Sabbath is, literally, as the term imports, a day of rest, and not a day of religious labour. They farther argue, that religion was bestowed upon man, not to lessen, but to augment his happiness—and that it ought therefore to infuse a spirit of cheerfulness and hilarity into the mind—for cheerfulness is the twin-sister of religion.

Last evening, as I entered my room, after a visit to two noble packet ships just arrived from New-York, which as nearly resemble "floating palaces" as any thing not described in the Arabian tales well can—I discovered, lying upon my table, a ticket for the American or Camp-street theatre, folded in a narrow slip of a play-bill, which informed me that the laughable entertainment of the "Three Hunchbacks," with the interesting play of "Cinderella," was to constitute the performance of the night: Cinderella, that tale which, with Blue Beard, the Forty Thieves, and some others, has such charms for children, and which, represented on the stage, has the power to lead stern man, with softened feelings, back to infancy. In a few moments afterward my Boston friend, who had left the ticket in my room, came in with another for the French theatre, giving me a choice between the two. I decided upon attending both, dividing the evening between them. After tea we sallied out, in company with half of those who were at the supper-table, on our way to the theatre. The street and adjacent buildings shone brilliantly, with the glare of many lamps suspended from the theatre and coffee houses in the vicinity. A noisy crowd was gathered around the ticket-office—the side-walks were filled with boys and negroes—and the curb-stone was lined with coloured females, each surrounded by bonbons, fruit, nuts, cakes, pies, gingerbread, and all the other et cetera of a "cake-woman's commodity." Entering the theatre, which is a plain handsome edifice, with a stuccoed front, and ascending a broad flight of steps, we passed across the first lobby, down a narrow aisle, opened through the centre of the boxes into the pit or *parquette*, as it is here termed, which is considered the most eligible and fashionable part of the house. This is rather reversing the order of things as found with us at the north. The pews, or slips—for the internal arrangement, were precisely like those of a church—were cushioned with crimson materials, and filled with bonnetless ladies, with their heads dressed *à la Madonna*. We seated ourselves near the orchestra. The large green curtain still concealed the mimic world behind it; and I embraced the few moments of delay previous to its rising, to gaze upon this Thespian temple of the south, and a New Orleans audience.

The "parquette" was brilliant with bright eyes and pretty faces; and upon the bending galaxy of ladies which glittered in the front of the boxes around it, I seemed to gaze through the medium of a rainbow. There were, it must be confessed, some plain enough faces among them; but, at the first glance of the eye, one might verily have believed himself encircled by a gallery of houris. The general character of their faces was decidedly American; exactly such as one gazes upon at the Tremont or Park theatre; and I will henceforward eschew physiognomy, if "I guess" would not have dropped more naturally from the lips of one half who were before me, while conversing, than "I reckon." There were but few French faces among the females; but, with two or three exceptions, these were extremely pretty. Most of the delicately-reared Creoles, or Louisianian ladies, are eminently beautiful. A Psyche-like fascination slumbers in their dark, eloquent eyes, whose richly fringed lids droop timidly over them—softening but not diminishing their brilliance. Their style of beauty is *unique,* and not easily classed. It is neither French nor English, but a combination of both, mellowed and enriched under a southern sky.—They are just such creatures as Vesta and Venus would have moulded, had they united to form a faultless woman.

The interior of the house was richly decorated; and the panelling in the interior of the boxes was composed of massive mirror-plates, multiplying the audience with a fine effect. The stage was lofty, extensive, and so constructed, either intentionally or accidentally, as to reflect the voice with unusual precision and distinctness. The scenery was in general well executed: one of the forest scenes struck me as remarkably true to nature, both in colouring and design. While surveying the gaudy interior, variegated with gilding, colouring, and mirrors, the usual cry of "Down, down?—Hats off," warned us to be seated. The performance was good for the pieces represented. The company, with the indefatigable Caldwell at its head, is strong and of a respectable character. When the second act was concluded we left the house; and passing through a parti-coloured mob, gathered around the entrance, and elbowing a gens d'armes or two, stationed in the lobby *in terrorem* to the turbulent—we gained the street, amidst a shouting of "Your check, sir! your check!—Give me your check—Please give me your check!—check!—check!—check!" from a host of boys, who knocked one another about unmercifully in their exertions to secure the prizes, which, to escape a mobbing, we threw into the midst of them; and jumping into a carriage in waiting, drove off to the French theatre, leaving them embroiled in a *pêle mêle,* in which the sciences of phlebotomy and phrenology were "being" tested by very practical applications.

After a drive of half a league or more through long and narrow streets, dimly lighted by swinging lamps, we were set down at the door of the Theatre d'Orleans, around which a crowd was assembled of as different a character, from that we had just escaped, as would have met our eyes had we been deposited before the *Theatre Royale* in Paris. The street was illuminated from the brilliantly lighted cafés and cabarets, clustered around this "nucleus" of gayety and amusement. As we crossed the broad *pavé* into the vestibule of the theatre, the rapidly enunciated, nasal sounds of the French language assailed our ears from every side. Ascending the stairs and entering the boxes, I was struck with the liveliness and brilliancy of the scene, which the interior exhibited to the eye. "Magnificent!" was upon my lips—but a moment's observation convinced me that its brilliancy was an illusion, created by numerous lights, and an artful arrangement and lavish display of gilding and colouring. The whole of the interior, including the stage decorations and scenic effect, was much inferior to that of the house we had just quitted. The boxes—if caverns resembling the interior of a ship's long-boat, with one end elevated three feet, and equally convenient, can be so called—were cheerless and uncomfortable. There were but few females in the house, and none of these were in the pit, as at the other theatre. Among them I saw but two or three pretty faces; and evidently none were of the first class of French society in this city. The house was thinly attended, presenting, wherever I turned my eyes, a "beggarly account of empty boxes." I found that I had chosen a night, of all others, the least calculated to give me a good idea of a French audience, in a cis-Atlantic French theatre. After remaining half an hour, wearied with a tiresome *ritornello* of a popular French air—listening with the devotion of a "Polytechnique" to the blood-stirring Marseillaise hymn—amused at the closing scene of a laughable comédie, and edified by the first of a pantomime, and observing, that with but one lovely exception, the Mesdames *du scêne* were very plain, and the Messieurs very handsome, we left the theatre and returned to our hotel, whose deserted bar-room, containing here and there a straggler, presented a striking contrast to the noise and bustle of the multitude by which it was thronged at noon-day. In general, strangers consider the *tout ensemble* of this theatre on Sabbath evenings, and on others when the élite of the New-Orleans society is collected there, decidedly superior to that of any other in the United States.

Beside the theatres there are other public buildings in this city, deserving the attention of a stranger, whose institution generally reflects the highest eulogium upon individuals, and the public. The effects of the benevolence of the generous M. Poydras, will for ever remain monuments of his piety and of the nobleness of his nature. Generation after generation will rise up from the bosom of this great city and "call him blessed." The charitable institutions of this city are lights which redeem the darker shades of its moral picture. Regarded as originators of benevolence, carried out into efficient operation, the Orleanese possess a moral beauty in their character as citizens and men, infinitely transcending that of many other cities ostensibly living under a higher code of morals. In the male and female orphan asylums, which are distinct institutions, endowed by the donations of M. Poydras—in a library for the use of young men, and in her hospitals and various charitable institutions, mostly sustained by Roman Catholic influence and patronage, whose doors are ever open to the stranger and the moneyless—the poor and the lame—the halt and the blind—and unceasingly send forth, during the fearful scourges which lay waste this ill-fated city, angels of mercy in human forms to heal the sick—comfort the dying—bind up the broken-hearted—feed the hungry, and clothe the naked—in these institutions—the ever living monuments of her humanity—New-Orleans, reviled as she has been abroad, holds a high rank among the cities of Christendom.

An original and able writer, with one or two extracts from whom I will conclude this letter, in allusion to this city says—"the French here, as elsewhere, display their characteristic urbanity and politeness, and are the same gay, dancing, spectacle-loving people, that they are found to be in every other place. There is, no doubt, much gambling and dissipation practised here, and different licensed gambling houses pay a large tax for their licenses. Much has been said abroad about the profligacy of manners and morals here. Amidst such a multitude, composed in a great measure of the low people of all nations, there must of course be much debauchery and low vice. But all the disgusting forms of vice, debauchery and drunkenness, are assorted together in their own place. Each man has an elective attraction to men of his own standing and order.

"This city necessarily exercises a very great influence over all the western country. There is no distinguished merchant, or planter, or farmer, in the Mississippi valley, who has not made at least one trip to this place. Here they see acting at the French and American theatres. Here they go to see at least, if not to take a part in, the pursuits of the "roulette and temple of Fortune." Here they come from the remote and isolated points of the west to behold the "city lions," and learn the ways of men in great towns; and they necessarily carry back an impression, from what they have seen, and heard. It is of inconceivable importance to the western country, that New-Orleans should be enlightened, moral, and religious. It has a numerous and respectable corps of professional men, and issues a considerable number of well edited papers.

"The police of the city is at once mild and energetic. Notwithstanding the multifarious character of the people, collected from every country and every climate, notwithstanding the multitude of boatmen and sailors, notwithstanding the mass of the people that rushes along the streets is of the most incongruous materials, there are fewer broils and quarrels here than in almost any other city. The municipal and the criminal courts are prompt in administering justice, and larcenies and broils are effectually punished without any just grounds of complaint about the "law's delay." On the whole we conclude, that the morals of those people, who profess to have any degree of self-respect, are not behind those of the other cities of the Union.

"Much has been said abroad, in regard to the unhealthiness of this city; and the danger of a residence here for an unacclimated person has been exaggerated. This circumstance, more than all others, has retarded its increase. The chance of an unacclimated young man from the north, for surviving the first summer, is by some considered only as one to two. Unhappily, when the dog-star is in the sky, there is but too much probability that the epidemic will sweep the place with the besom of destruction. Hundreds of the unacclimated poor from the north, and more than half from Ireland, fall victims to it. But the city is now furnished with noble water works; and is in this way supplied with the healthy and excellent water of the river. Very great improvements have been recently made and are constantly making, in paving the city, in removing the wooden sewers, and replacing them by those of stone. The low places, where the waters used to stagnate, are drained, or filled up. Tracts of swamp about the town are also draining, or filling up; and this work, constantly pursued, will probably contribute more to the salubrity of the city, than all the other efforts to this end united."

XXII

This is the last day of my sojourn in the great emporium of the south-west. To-morrow will find me threading the majestic sinuosities of the Mississippi, the prisoner of one of its mammoth steamers, on my way to the state whose broad fields and undulating hills are annually whitened with the fleece-like cotton, and whose majestic forests glitter with the magnificent and silvery magnolia—where the men are chivalrous, generous, and social, and the women so lovely,

— — "that the same lips and eyes
They wear on earth will serve in Paradise."

A gentleman to whom I brought a letter of introduction called yesterday—a strange thing for men so honoured to do—and invited me to ride with him to his plantation, a few miles from the city. He drove his own phaeton, which was drawn by two beautiful long-tailed bays. After a drive of a mile and a half, we cleared the limits of the straggling, and apparently interminable faubourgs, and, emerging through a long narrow street upon the river road, bounded swiftly over its level surface, which was as smooth as a bowling-green—saving a mud-hole now and then, where a crevasse had let in upon it a portion of the Mississippi. An hour's drive, after clearing the suburbs, past a succession of isolated villas, encircled by slender columns and airy galleries, and surrounded by richly foliaged gardens, whose fences were bursting with the luxuriance which they could scarcely confine, brought us in front of a charming residence situated at the head of a broad, gravelled avenue, bordered by lemon and orange trees, forming in the heat of summer, by arching naturally overhead, a cool and shady promenade. We drew up at the massive gateway and alighted. As we entered the avenue, three or four children were playing at its farther extremity, with noise enough for Christmas holidays; two of them were trundling hoops in a race, and a third sat astride of a non-locomotive wooden horse, waving a tin sword, and charging at half a dozen young slaves, who were testifying their bellicose feelings by dancing and shouting around him with the noisiest merriment.

"Pa! pa!" shouted the hoop-drivers as they discovered our approach—"Oh, there's pa!" re-echoed the pantalette dragoon, dismounting from his dull steed, and making use of his own chubby legs as the most speedy way of advancing, "oh, my papa!"—and, sword and hoops in hand, down they all came upon the run to meet us, followed helter-skelter by their ebony troop, who scattered the gravel around them like hail as they raced, turning summersets over each other, without much diminution of their speed. They came down upon us altogether with such momentum, that we were like to be carried from our feet by this novel charge of *infantry* and laid *hors du combat,* upon the ground. The playful and affectionate congratulations over between the noble little fellows and their parent, we walked toward the house, preceded by our trundlers, with the young soldier hand-in-hand between us, followed close behind by the little Africans, whose round shining eyes glistened wishfully—speaking as plainly as eyes could speak the strong desire, with which their half-naked limbs evidently sympathized by their restless motions, to bound ahead, contrary to decorum, "wid de young massas!"

Around the semi-circular flight of steps, ascending to the piazza of the dwelling,—the columns of which were festooned with the golden jasmine and luxuriant multiflora,—stood, in large green vases, a variety of flowers, among which I observed the tiny flowerets of the diamond myrtle, sparkling like crystals of snow, scattered upon rich green leaves—the dark foliaged Arabian jasmine silvered with its opulently-leaved flowers redolent of the sweetest perfume,—and the rose-geranium, breathing gales of fragrance upon the air. From this point the main avenue branches to the right and left, into narrower, yet not less beautiful walks, which, lined with evergreen and flowering shrubs, completely encircled the cottage. At the head of the flight of steps which led from this Hesperean spot to the portico, we were met by a little golden-haired fairy, as light in her motion as a zephyr, and with a cheek—not alabaster, indeed, for that is an exotic in the south—but like a lily, shaded by a rose leaf, and an eye of the purest hue, melting in its own light. With an exclamation of delight she sprang into her father's arms. I was soon seated upon one of the settees in the piazza,—whose front and sides were festooned by the folds of a green curtain—in a high frolic with the trundlers, the dismounted dragoon and my little winged zephyr. You know my *penchant* for children's society. I am seldom happier than when watching a group of intelligent and beautiful little ones at play. For those who can in after life enter *con amore,* into the sports of children, tumble with and be tumbled about by them, it is like living their childhood over again. Every romp with them is death to a score of gray hairs. Their games, moreover, present such a contrast to the rougher contests of bearded children in the game of life, where money, power, and ambition are the stake, that it is refreshing to look at them and mingle with them, even were it only to realize that human nature yet retains something of its divine original.

The proprietor of the delightful spot which lay spread out around me—a lake of foliage—fringed by majestic forest trees, and diversified with labyrinthyne walks,—had, the preceding summer, consigned to the tomb the mother of his "beautiful ones." They were under the care of a dignified lady, his sister, and the widow of a gentleman formerly distinguished as a lawyer in New-England. But like many other northern ladies, whose names confer honour upon our literature, and whose talents elevate and enrich our female seminaries of education, she had independence enough to rise superior to her widowed indigence; and had prepared to open a boarding school at the north, when the death of his wife led her wealthier brother to invite her to supply a mother's place to his children, to whom she was now both mother and governess. The history of this lady is that of hundreds of her country-women. There are, I am informed, many instances in the south-west, of New-England's daughters having sought, with the genuine spirit of independence, thus to repair their broken fortunes. The intelligent and very agreeable lady of the late President H., of Lexington, resides in the capacity of governess in a distinguished Louisianian family, not far from the city. Mrs. Thayer, formerly an admired poet and an interesting writer of fiction, is at the head of a seminary in an adjoining state. And in the same, the widow of the late president of its college is a private instructress in the family of a planter. And these are instances, to which I can add many others, in a country where the occupation of instructing, whether invested in the president of a college or in the teacher of a country school, is degraded to a secondary rank. In New-England, on the contrary, the lady of a living collegiate president is of the élite, decidedly, if not at the head, of what is there termed "good society." Here, the same lady, whether a visiter for the winter, or a settled resident, must yield in rank—as the laws of southern society have laid it down—to the lady of the planter. The southerners, however, when they can secure one of our well-educated northern ladies in their families, know well how to appreciate their good fortune. Inmates of the family, they are treated with politeness and kindness; but in the soirée, dinner party, or levée, the governess is thrown more into the back-ground than she would be in a gentleman's family, even in aristocratic England; and her title to an equality with the gay, and fashionable, and wealthy circle by whom she is surrounded, and her challenge to the right of *caste*, is less readily admitted. But this illiberal jealousy is the natural consequence of the crude state of American society, where the line of demarcation between its rapidly forming classes is yet so uncertainly defined, that each individual who is anxious to be, or even to be thought, of the better file, has to walk circumspectly, lest he should inadvertently be found mingling with the *canaille*. The more uncertain any individual is of his own true standing, the more haughtily and suspiciously will he stand aloof, and measure with his eye every stranger who advances within the limits of the prescribed circle.

Education in this state has been and is still very much neglected. Appropriations have been made for public schools; but, from the fund established for the purpose, not much has as yet been effected. Many of the males, after leaving the city-schools, or the care of tutors, are sent, if destined for a professional career, to the northern colleges; others to the Catholic institutions at St. Louis and Bardstown, and a few of the wealthier young gentlemen to France. The females are educated, either by governesses, at the convents, or at northern boarding-schools. Many of them are sent to Paris when very young, and there remain until they have completed their education. The majority of the higher classes of the French population are brought up there. This custom of foreign education—like that in the Atlantic states, under the old regime, when, to be educated a gentleman, it was considered necessary for American youth to enter at Eton, and graduate from Oxford or Cambridge—must have a very natural tendency to preserve and cherish an attachment for France, seriously detrimental to genuine patriotism.—But all this is a digression.

After a kind of bachelor's dinner, in a hall open on two sides for ventilation, even at this season of the year—sumptuous enough for Epicurus, and served by two or three young slaves, who were drilled to a glance of the eye—crowned by a luxurious dessert of fruits and sweet-meats, and graced with wine, not of the *chasse-cousin vintage*, so common in New England, but of the pure *outre-mer*—we proceeded to the sugar-house or *sucrérie*, through a lawn which nearly surrounded the ornamental grounds about the house, studded here and there with lofty trees, which the good taste of the original proprietor of the domain had left standing in their forest majesty. From this rich green sward, on which two or three fine saddle-horses were grazing, we passed through a turn-stile into a less lovely, but more domestic enclosure, alive with young negroes, sheep, turkeys, hogs, and every variety of domestic animal that could be attached to a plantation. From this diversified collection, which afforded a tolerable idea of the interior of Noah's ark, we entered the long street of a village of white cottages, arranged on either side of it with great regularity. They were all exactly alike, and separated by equal spaces; and to every one was attached an enclosed piece of ground, apparently for a vegetable garden; around the doors decrepit and superannuated negroes were basking in the evening sun—mothers were nursing their naked babies, and one or two old and blind negresses were spinning in their doors. In the centre of the street, which was a hundred yards in width, rose to the height of fifty feet a framed belfry, from whose summit was suspended a bell, to regulate the hours of labour. At the foot of this tower, scattered over the grass, lay half a score of black children, *in puris naturalibus*, frolicking or sleeping in the warm sun, under the surveillance of an old African matron, who sat knitting upon a camp-stool in the midst of them.

We soon arrived at the boiling-house, which was an extensive brick building with tower-like chimneys, numerous flues, and a high, steep roof, reminding me of a New England distillery. As we entered, after scaling a barrier of sugar-casks with which the building was surrounded, the slaves, who were dressed in coarse trowsers, some with and others without shirts, were engaged in the several departments of their sweet employment; whose fatigues some African Orpheus was lightening with a loud chorus, which was instantly hushed, or rather modified, on our entrance, to a half-assured whistling. A white man, with a very unpleasing physiognomy, carelessly leaned against one of the brick pillars, who raised his hat very respectfully as we passed, but did not change his position. This was the overseer. He held in his hand a short-handled whip, loaded in the butt, which had a lash four or five times the length of the staff. Without noticing us, except when addressed by his employer, he remained watching the motions of the toiling slaves, quickening the steps of a loiterer by a word, or threatening with his whip, those who, tempted by curiosity, turned to gaze after us, as we walked through the building.

The process of sugar-making has been so often described by others, that I can offer nothing new or interesting upon the subject. But since my visit to this plantation, I have fallen in with an ultra-montane tourist or sketcher, a fellow-townsman and successful practitioner of medicine in Louisiana, who has kindly presented me with the sheet of an unpublished MS. which I take pleasure in transcribing, for the very graphic and accurate description it conveys of this interesting process.

"The season of sugar-making," says Dr. P. "is termed, by the planters of the south, the 'rolling season;' and a merry and pleasant time it is too—for verily, as Paulding says, the making of sugar and the making of love are two of the sweetest occupations in this world. It commences—the making of sugar I mean—about the middle or last of October, and continues from three weeks to as many months, according to the season and other circumstances; but more especially the force upon the plantation, and the amount of sugar to be made. As the season approaches, every thing assumes a new and more cheerful aspect. The negroes are more animated, as their winter clothing is distributed, their little crops are harvested, and their wood and other comforts secured for that season; which, to them, if not the freest, is certainly the gayest and happiest portion of the year. As soon as the corn crop and fodder are harvested, every thing is put in motion for the grinding. The horses and oxen are increased in number and better groomed; the carts and other necessary utensils are overhauled and repaired, and some hundred or thousand cords of wood are cut and ready piled for the manufacture of the sugar. The *sucrérie*, or boiling house, is swept and garnished—the mill and engine are polished—the kettles scoured—the coolers caulked, and the *purgerie*, or draining-house, cleaned and put in order, where the casks are arranged to receive the sugar.

The first labour in anticipation of grinding, is that of providing plants for the coming year; and this is done by cutting the cane, and putting it in *matelas*, or mattressing it, as it is commonly called. The cane is cut and thrown into parcels in different parts of the field, in quantities sufficient to plant several acres, and so arranged that the tops of one layer may completely cover and protect the stalks of another. After the quantity required is thus secured, the whole plantation force, nearly, is employed in cutting cane, and conveying it to the mill. The cane is divested of its tops, which are thrown aside, unless they are needed for plants, which is often the case, when they are thrown together in rows, and carefully protected from the inclemencies of the weather. The stalks are then cut as near as may be to the ground, and thrown into separate parcels or rows, to be taken to the mill in carts, and expressed as soon as possible. The cane is sometimes bound together in bundles, in the field, which facilitates its transportation, and saves both time and trouble. As soon as it is harvested, it is placed upon a cane-carrier, so called, which conveys it to the mill, where it is twice expressed between iron rollers, and made perfectly dry. The juice passes into vats, or receivers, and the *baggasse* or cane-trash, (called in the West Indies *migass*,) is received into carts and conveyed to a distance from the sugar-house to be burnt as soon as may be. Immediately after the juice is expressed, it is distributed to the boilers, generally four in succession, ranged in solid masonry along the sides of the boiling-room, where it is properly tempered, and its purification and evaporation are progressively advanced. The French have commonly five boilers, distinguished by the fanciful names of *grande—propre—flambeau—sirop*, and *battérie*.

In the first an alkali is generally put to temper the juice; lime is commonly used, and the quantity is determined by the good judgment and experience of the sugar-maker. In the last kettle—the *teach* as it is termed—the sugar is concentrated to the granulating point, and then conveyed into coolers, which hold from two to three hogsheads. After remaining here for twenty-four hours or more, it is removed to the *purgerie*, or draining-house, and placed in hogsheads, which is technically called *potting*. Here it undergoes the process of draining for a few days or weeks, and is then ready for the market. The molasses is received beneath in cisterns, and when they become filled, it is taken out and conveyed into barrels or hogsheads and shipped. When all the molasses is removed from the cistern, an inferior kind of sugar is re-manufactured, which is called *cistern-sugar*, and sold at a lower price. When the grinding has once commenced, there is no cessation of labour till it is completed. From beginning to end, a busy and cheerful scene continues. The negroes

> "—— Whose sore task
> Does not divide the Sunday from the week,"

work from eighteen to twenty hours,

> "And make the night joint-labourer with the day."

Though to lighten the burden as much as possible, the gang is divided into two watches, one taking the first, and the other the last part of the night; and notwithstanding this continued labour, the negroes improve in condition, and appear fat and flourishing. "They drink freely of cane-juice, and the sickly among them revive and become robust and healthy." After the grinding is finished, the negroes have several holidays, when they are quite at liberty to dance and frolic as much as they please; and the cane-song—which is improvised by one of the gang, the rest all joining in a prolonged and unintelligible chorus—now breaks night and day upon the ear, in notes "most musical, most melancholy." This over, planting recommences, and the same routine of labour is continued, with an intermission—except during the boiling season, as above stated—upon most, if not all plantations, of twelve hours in twenty-four, and of one day in seven throughout the year.

Leaving the sugar-house, after having examined some of the most interesting parts of the process so well described by Dr. P., I returned with my polite entertainer to the house. Lingering for a moment on the gallery in the rear of the dwelling-house, I dwelt with pleasure upon the scene which the domain presented.

The lawn, terminated by a snow-white paling, and ornamented here and there by a venerable survivor of the aboriginal forest, was rolled out before me like a carpet, and dotted with sleek cows, and fine horses, peacefully grazing, or indolently reclining upon the thick grass, chewing the cud of contentment. Beyond the lawn, and extending farther into the plantation, lay a pasture containing a great number of horses and cattle, playing together, reposing, feeding, or standing in social clusters around a shaded pool. Beyond, the interminable cane-field, or plantation proper, spread away without fence or swell, till lost in the distant forests which bounded the horizon. On my left, a few hundred yards from the house, and adjoining the pasture, stood the stables and other plantation appurtenances, constituting a village in themselves—for planters always have a separate building for everything. To the right stood the humble yet picturesque village or "quarter" of the slaves, embowered in trees, beyond which, farther toward the interior of the plantation, arose the lofty walls and turreted chimneys of the sugar-house, which, combined with the bell-tower, presented the appearance of a country village with its church-tower and the walls of some public edifice, lifting themselves above the trees. Some of the sugar-houses are very lofty and extensive, with noble wings and handsome fronts, resembling—aside from their lack of windows—college edifices. I have seen two which bore a striking resemblance, as seen from the river, to the Insane Hospital near Boston. It requires almost a fortune to construct one. The whole scene before me was extremely animated. Human figures were moving in all directions over the place. Some labouring in the distant field, others driving the slow-moving oxen, with a long, drawling cry—half naked negro boys shouting and yelling, were galloping horses as wild as themselves—negresses of all sizes, from one able to carry a tub to the minikin who could "tote" but a pint-dipper, laughing and chattering as they went, were conveying water from a spring to the wash-house, in vessels adroitly balanced upon their heads. Slaves sinking under pieces of machinery, and other burdens, were passing and repassing from the boiling-house and negro quarter. Some were calling to others afar off, and the merry shouts of the black children at their sports in their village, reminding me of a school just let out, mingled with the lowing of cows, the cackling of geese, the bleating of lambs, the loud and unmusical clamour of the guinea-hen, agreeably varied by the barking of dogs, and the roaring of some young African rebel under maternal castigation.

Passing from this plantation scene through the airy hall of the dwelling, which opened from piazza to piazza through the house, to the front gallery, whose light columns were wreathed with the delicately leaved Cape-jasmine, rambling woodbine and honeysuckle, a lovelier and more agreeable scene met my eye. I stood almost embowered in the foliage of exotics and native plants, which stood upon the gallery in handsome vases of marble and China-ware. The main avenue opened a vista to the river through a paradise of althea, orange, lemon, and olive trees, and groves and lawns extended on both sides of this lovely spot,

"Where Flora's brightest broidery shone,"

terminating at the villas of adjoining plantations. The Mississippi—always majestic and lake-like in its breadth—rolled past her turbid flood, dotted here and there by a market-lugger, with its black crew and clumsy sails. By the Levée, on the opposite shore, lay a brig, taking in a cargo of sugar from the plantation, whose noble colonnaded mansion rose like a palace above its low, grove-lined margin, and an English argosy of great size, with black spars and hull, was moving under full sail down the middle of the river. As I was under the necessity of returning to the city the same evening, I took leave of the youthful family of my polite host, who clustered around us as we walked along the avenue to the gateway, endeavouring to detain us till the next morning. The young rogue of a dragoon, who was now metamorphosed into a trumpeter—what a singular propensity little chubby boys have for the weapons and apparel of war!—a most mischievous little cupidon of but two or three summers' growth, was very desirous of accompanying us to town, on seeing us seated in the carriage; but finding that his eloquent appeals were unheeded, he took a fancy to a noble pointer, spotted like a leopard, which accompanied me, and clinging around the neck of the majestic and docile creature, as we drove from the gate, said in a half playful, half pettish tone, "Me ride dis pretty dog-horse, den." The sensible animal stood like a statue till the little fellow relaxed his embrace, when he darted after the carriage, then a quarter of a mile from the gate, bounding like a stag. The cries of "Pa, bring me this," and "Pa, bring me that," were soon lost in the distance, and rolling like the wind over the level road along the banks of the river, we arrived in the city and alighted at Bishop's a few minutes after seven.

XXIII

Once more I am floating upon the "Father of rivers." New-Orleans, with its crowd of "mingled nations", is seen indistinctly in the distance. We are now doubling a noble bend in the river, which will soon hide the city from our sight; but scenes of rural enchantment are opening before us as we advance, which will amply and delightfully repay us for its absence.

What a splendid panorama of opulence and beauty is now spread out around us! Sublimity is wanting to make the painting perfect—but its picturesque effect is unrivalled.

Below us a few miles, indistinctly seen through the haze, a dense forest of masts, and here and there a tower, designate the emporium of commerce—the key of the mighty west. The banks are lined and ornamented with elegant mansions, displaying, in their richly adorned grounds, the wealth and taste of their possessors; while the river, now moving onward like a golden flood, reflecting the mellow rays of the setting sun, is full of life. Vessels of every size are gliding in all directions over its waveless bosom, while graceful skiffs dart merrily about like white-winged birds. Huge steamers are dashing and thundering by, leaving long trains of wreathing smoke in their rear. Carriages filled with ladies and attended by gallant horsemen, enliven the smooth road along the Levée; while the green banks of the Levée itself are covered with gay promenaders. A glimpse through the trees now and then, as we move rapidly past the numerous villas, detects the piazzas, filled with the young, beautiful, and aged of the family, enjoying the rich beauty of the evening, and of the objects upon which my own eyes rest with admiration.

The scene has changed. The moon rides high in the east, while the western star hangs trembling in the path of the sun. Innumerable lights twinkle along the shores, or flash out from some vessel as we glide rapidly past. How exhilarating to be upon the water by moonlight! But a snow-white sail, a graceful barque, and a woodland lake—with a calm, clear, moonlight, sleeping upon it like a blessing—must be marshalled for poetical effect. There is nothing of that here. Quiet and romance are lost in sublimity, if not in grandeur. The great noise of rushing waters—the deep-toned booming of the steamer—the fearful rapidity with which we are borne past the half-obscured objects on shore and in the stream—the huge columns of black smoke rolling from the mouths of the gigantic chimneys, and spangled with showers of sparks, flying like trains of meteors shooting through the air; while a proud consciousness of the power of the dark hull beneath your feet, which plunges, thundering onward—a thing of majesty and life—adds to the majesty and wonder of the time.

The passengers have descended to the cabin; some to turn in, a few to read, but more to play at the ever-ready card-table. The pilot (as the helmsman is here termed) stands in his lonely wheel-house, comfortably enveloped in his blanket-coat—the hurricane deck is deserted, and the hands are gathered in the bows, listening to the narration of some ludicrous adventure of recent transaction in the city of hair-breadth escapes. Now and then a laugh from the merry auditors, or a loud roar from some ebony-cheeked fireman, as he pitches his wood into the gaping furnace, breaks upon the stillness of night, startling the echoes along the shores. What beings of habit we are! How readily do we accustom ourselves to circumstances! The deep trombone of the steam-pipe—the regular splash of the paddles—and the incessant rippling of the water eddying away astern, as our noble vessel flings it from her sides, no longer affect the senses, unless it may be to lull them into a repose well meant for contemplation. They are now no longer auxiliaries to the scene—habit has made them a part of it: and I can pace the deck with my mind as free and undisturbed as though I were in a lonely boat, upon "the dark blue sea", with no sound but the beating of my own heart, to break the silence. A few short hours have passed, and the grander characters of the scene are mellowed down, by their familiarity with my senses, into calm and quiet loneliness.

Having secured a berth in one corner of the spacious cabin, where I could draw the rich crimsoned curtains around me, and with book or pen pass my time somewhat removed from the bustle, and undisturbed by the constant passing of the restless passengers, I began this morning to look about me upon my fellow-travellers, seeking familiar faces, or scanning strange ones, by Lavater's doubtful rules.

Our passengers are a strange medley, not only representing every state and territory washed by this great river, but nearly every Atlantic and trans-Atlantic state and nation. In the cabin are the merchants and planters of the "up country;" and on deck, emigrants, return-boatmen, &c. &c. I may say something more of them hereafter, but not at present, as the scenery through which we are passing is too attractive to keep me longer below. So, to the deck. We are now about sixty miles above New-Orleans, and the shores have presented, the whole distance, one continued line of noble mansions, some of them princely and magnificent, intermingled, at intervals, with humbler farm-houses.

I think I have remarked, in a former letter, that the plantations along the river extend from the Levée to the swamps in the rear; the distance across the belt of land being, from the irregular encroachment of the marshes, from one to two or three miles. These plantations have been, for a very long period, under cultivation for the production of sugar crops. As the early possessor of large tracts of land had sons to settle, they portioned off parallelograms to each; which, to combine the advantages of exportation and wood, extended from the river to the flooded forest in the rear. These, in time, portioned off to their children, while every occupant of a tract erected his dwelling at the head of his domain, one or two hundred yards from the river. Other plantations retain their original dimensions, crowned, on the borders of the river, with noble mansions, embowered in the evergreen foliage of the dark-leaved orange and lemon trees. The shores, consequently, present, from the lofty deck of a steamer,—from which can be had an extensive prospect of the level country—a very singular appearance.

Farm-houses thickly set, or now and then separated by a prouder structure, line the shores with tasteful parterres and shady trees around them; while parallel lines of fence, commencing at these cottages, frequently but a few rods apart, extend away into the distance, till the numerous lines dwindle apparently to a point, and present the appearance of radii diverging from one common centre. A planter thus may have a plantation a league in length, though not a furlong in breadth. The regularity of these lines, the flatness of the country, and the *fac simile* farm-houses, render the scenery in general rather monotonous; though some charming spots, that might have been stolen from Paradise, fully atone for the wearisome character of the rest. We have passed several Catholic churches, prettily situated, surrounded by the white monuments of the dead. On our right, the lofty walls of a huge edifice, just completed, and intended for a university, rear themselves in the midst of a vast plain, once an extensive sugar plantation. This embryo institution is under state patronage. It is a noble brick building, advantageously situated for health, beauty, and convenience; and calculated, from its vast size, to accommodate a large number of students. It is to be of a sectarian character, devoted, I understand, to the interest of the Roman church.

A mile above, the towers and crosses of a pile of buildings, half hidden by a majestic grove of noble forest trees, attract the attention of the traveller. They are the convent du Sacré Cœur,—the nursery of the fair daughters of Louisiana. There are two large buildings, exclusive of the chapel and the residence of the officiating priest. The site is eminently beautiful, and, compared with the general tameness of the scenery in this region, romantic. A padre, in his long black gown, is promenading the Levée, and the windows of the convent are relieved by the presence of figures, which, the spy-glass informs us, are those of the fair prisoners; who, perhaps with many a sigh, are watching the rapid motion of our boat, with its busy, bustling scene on board, contrasting it with their incarcerated state, probably inducing reflections of a melancholy cast, with ardent aspirations for the "wings of a dove."

The education of females is well attended to in this state; though the peculiar doctrines of the Roman Catholic church are inculcated with their tasks.

The villages of Plaquemine and Donaldsonville, the latter formerly the seat of government, are pleasant, quiet, and rural. The latter is distinguished by a dilapidated state-house, which lifts itself above the humbler dwellings around it, and adds much to the importance and beauty of the town in the eye of the traveller as he sails past. But the streets of the village are solitary; and closed stores and deserted taverns add to their loneliness. Between New-Orleans and Baton Rouge, a distance of one hundred and seventeen miles, the few villages upon the river all partake, more or less, of this humble and dilapidated character. Baton Rouge is now in sight, a few miles above. As we approach it the character of the scene changes. Hills once more relieve the eye, so long wearied with gazing upon a flat yet beautiful country. These are the first hills that gladden the sight of the traveller as he ascends the river. They are to the northerner like oases in a desert. How vividly and how agreeably does the sight of their green slopes, and graceful undulations, conjure up the loved and heart-cherished scenes of home!

We are now nearly opposite the town, which is pleasantly situated upon the declivity of the hill, retreating over its brow and spreading out on a plain in the rear, where the private dwellings are placed, shaded and half embowered in the rich foliage of that loveliest of all shade-trees, "the pride of China." The stores and other places of business are upon the front street, which runs parallel with the river. The site of the town is about forty feet above the highest flood, and rises by an easy and gentle swell from the water. The barracks, a short distance from the village, are handsome and commodious, constructed around a pentagonal area—four noble buildings forming four sides, while the fifth is open, fronting upon the river. The buildings are brick, with lofty colonnades and double galleries running along the whole front. The columns are yellow-stuccoed, striking the eye with a more pleasing effect, than the red glare of brick. The view of these noble structures from the river, as we passed, was very fine. From the esplanade there is an extensive and commanding prospect of the inland country—the extended shores, stretching out north and south, dotted with elegant villas, and richly enamelled by their high state of cultivation. The officers are gentlemanly men, and form a valuable acquisition to the society of the neighbourhood. This station must be to them an agreeable sinecure. The town, from the hasty survey which I was enabled to make of it, must be a delightful residence. It is neat and well built; the French and Spanish style of architecture prevails. The view of the town from the deck of the steamer is highly beautiful. The rich, green swells rising gradually from the water—its pleasant streets, bordered with the umbrageous China tree—its colonnaded dwellings—its mingled town and rural scenery, and its pleasant suburbs, give it an air of quiet and novel beauty, such as one loves to gaze upon in old landscapes which the imagination fills with ideal images of its own.

The scenery now partakes of another character. The rich plantations, waving with green and golden crops of cane, are succeeded here and there by a cotton plantation, but more generally by untrodden forests, hanging over the banks, which are now for a hundred miles of one uniform character and height—being about twenty feet above the highest floods. Now and then a "squatter's" hut, instead of relieving, adds to the wild and dreary character of the scene. This class of men with their families, are usually in a most wretched and squalid condition. As they live exposed to the fatal, poisonous miasma of the swamp, their complexions are cadaverous, and their persons wasted by disease. They sell wood to the steamboats for a means of subsistence—seldom cultivating what little cleared land there may be around them. There are exceptions to this, however. Many become eventually purchasers of the tracts on which they are settled, and lay foundations for fine estates and future independence.

Loftus's height, a striking eminence crowned by Fort Adams, appears in the distance. It is a cluster of cliffs and hills nearly two hundred feet in height. The old fort can just be discerned with a glass, surmounting a natural platform, half way up the side of the most prominent hill. The works present the appearance of a few green mounds, and though defaced by time, still bear evidence of having been a military post. The position is highly commanding and romantic. The scenery around would be termed striking, even in Maine, that romantic land of rocks, and cliffs, and mountains. A small village is at the base of the hills, containing a few stores. Cotton is exported hence, and steamers are now at the landing taking it in.

As we were passing the place on our way up the river, a white signal was displayed from a pole held by some one standing on the shore. In a few moments we came abreast of the fort, and in obedience to the fluttering signal, our steamer rounded gracefully to, and put her jolly boat off for the expected passengers. The boat had scarcely touched the bank, before the boatmen at one leap gained the baggage which lay piled upon the Levée, and tumbling it helter-skelter into the bottom of the boat, as though for life and death, called out, so as to be heard far above the deafening noise of the rushing steam as it hissed from the pipe, "Come gentlemen, come, the boat's a-waiting." The new passengers had barely time to pass into the boat and balance themselves erect upon the thwarts, before, impelled by the nervous arms of the boatmen, she was cutting her way through the turbid waves to the steamer, which had been kept in her position against the strong current of the river, by an occasional revolution of her wheels. The instant she struck her side the boat was cleared immediately of "bag and baggage," at the "risk of the owners" truly—and the hurrying passengers had hardly gained a footing upon the guard, before the loud, brief command, "go ahead," was heard, followed by the tinkling of the engineer's bell, the dull groaning of the ponderous, labouring engine, and the heavy dash of the water, as strongly beaten by the vast fins of this huge "river monster."

APPENDIX

Note A

The following Statistical Tables, exhibiting Louisiana in a variety of comparative views, have been compiled principally from the elaborate tables of that valuable periodical—the American Almanac and Repository of Useful Knowledge—for the year 1835.

LOUISIANA

Latitude of New-Orleans,	29°	57′	45″ North.
Longitude in degrees	90	60	49 West.
	h.	m.	s.
Longitude in time,	6	0	27.3
Distance from Washington, 1203 miles.			

Relative size of Louisiana, 5.	Extent in square miles, 45,220.

NUMBER OF INHABITANTS TO A SQUARE MILE

In 1810.	In 1820.	In 1830.
1.6	3.2	4.4

RELATIVE POPULATION

In 1810.			In 1820.			In 1820.		
Free	Slave	Total	Free	Slave	Total	Free	Slave	Total
18	8	17	19	8	17	21	8	19

RATE OF INCREASE OF FREE AND SLAVE POPULATION

From 1800 to 1810.			From 1810 to 1820.			From 1820 to 1830.		
Free	Slave	Total	Free	Slave	Total	Free	Slave	Total
					p. ct.			
			373	2193.7	636	25.8	58.7	40.6

POPULATION OF LOUISIANA IN 1810

Free	Slaves	No. of free to 1 slave	Total
41,896	34,660	1.20	76,556

In 1820

84,343	69,064	1.22	153,407

In 1830

106,151	109,588	.96	215,739

VALUE OF IMPORTS IN THE YEAR ENDING SEPTEMBER 30, 1833

In American vessels	In foreign vessels	Total
$6,658,916	$2,931,589	$9,590,505

VALUE OF EXPORTS IN THE SAME YEAR

Domestic Produce	Foreign Produce	Total of Domestic and Foreign Produce
$16,133,457	$2,807,916	$18,941,373
.Tonnage, 1st January, 1834—61,171,Tons		

GOVERNMENT

	Salary
Edward D. White, Governor (elect); Jan. 1835 to Jan. 1839	$7,500
George Eustis, Secretary of State	2,500
F. Gardere, Treasurer; 4 per cent. on all moneys received.	
Louis Bringier, Surveyor General	800
Claudius Crozet, Civil Engineer	5,000
F. Gaiennie, Adjutant and Inspector General	2,000
E. Mazureau, Attorney General	2,000

Senate, 17 members, elected for two years. C. Derbigny, President.

House of Representatives, 50 members, elected for two years. A. Labranche, Speaker.

JUDICIARY

Judges of the Supreme Court.—George Matthews, Francis X. Martin, and Henry A. Bullard. Salary of each, $5,000.

Judge of the Criminal Court of the City of New-Orleans.—John F. Canonge.

Judges of the District Courts.—Salary of each $2,000.

Charles Watts,	1st district.
Benjamin Winchester,	2d district.
Charles Bushnell,	3d district.
R. N. Ogden,	4th district.
Seth Lewis,	5th district.
J. H. Johnson,	6th district.
J. H. Overton,	7th district.
Clark Woodruff,	8th district.

The Supreme Court sits in the city of New-Orleans, for the Eastern district of the state during the months of November, December, January, February, March, April, May, June, and July; and for the Northern district, at Opelousas and Attakapas, during the months of August, September, and October; and at Baton Rouge, commencing the 1st Monday in August. The district courts, with the exception of the courts in the first district, hold, in each parish, two sessions during the year, to try causes originally instituted before them, and appeals from the parish courts. The parish courts hold their regular sessions in each parish on the first Monday in each month. The courts in the first district, composed of the district, parish, and criminal courts, and courts of probate, are in session during the whole year, excepting the months of July, August, September, and October, in which they hold special courts when necessary.

BANKS

State of the banks, January 7, 1834, as given in a document laid before Congress, June 21, 1834.

NAME.	Capital stock paid in.	Bills in circulation.	Specie and specie funds.
Canal and Banking Company	3,998,200	951,780	297,451.21
City Bank	2,000,000	380,670	335,288.88
Commercial Bank	817,835	145,000	135,903.73
Union bank of Louisiana	5,500,000	1,281,000	291,587.87
Louisiana State Bank	1,248,720	428,470	546,125.34
Consolidated Association Bank	2,500,000	84,300	61,936.43
	$16,064,755	3,271,230	1,568,293.46
Estimated situation of the following banks.—no returns.			
Bank of Louisiana	4,000,000 }		
Bank of Orlealns	600,000 }		
Citizens' Bank of Louisiana	1,000,000 }	1,522,500	650,000.00
Mechanics' and Traders' Bank	2,000,000 }	-	-
Total	$23,664,755	4,793,730	2,218,293.46

The Union Bank of Louisiana has branches at the following places, viz. Thiboudeauville, Covington, Marshville, Vermillionville, St. Martinsville, Plaquemine, Natchitoches, and Clinton.

Interest. "Legal interest is 5 per cent. Conventional interest, as high as 10 per cent., is legal. Of our banks, none can charge higher than 9 per cent., and some of them not higher than 8. But if I lend $100, and the borrower gives me his note for $110, $120, $130, $140, or even $150, or more, with 10 per cent. interest from date, the law legalizes the transaction, and will not set aside any part of the claim on the plea of usury. In fact, money is considered here like any other article in the market, and the holder may ask what price he pleases for it."

INSURANCE COMPANIES

Merchants' Insurance Company of New-Orleans	$1,000,000
Phoenix Fire Insurance Co. of London—agent at New Orleans	1,000,000
Louisiana Slate Marine and File Insurance Co.	400,000
Western Marine and Fire Insurance Company	300,000
Louisiana Insurance Company	300,000
Mississippi Marine and Fire Insurance Company	300,000
New-Orleans Insurance Company	200,000

Pontchartrain Rail-road Company	250,000
Orleans Navigation Company	200,000
Barataria and Lafourche Canal Company	150,000

NEWSPAPERS

Louisiana was originally settled by the French; in 1762, it was ceded by France to Spain; near the end of the 18th century it was restored to France; in 1803, it was purchased by the United States; in 1804, the country now forming the state of Louisiana was formed into a territorial government under the name of the Territory of Orleans; and in 1812, it was admitted into the Union as a state.

Mr. Thomas, in his "History of Printing," remarks "that several printing-houses were opened at New-Orleans, and several newspapers were immediately published there, after the country came under the government of the United States."

The first paper published in New-Orleans was the "Moniteur de la Louisiana," a French paper, and edited by M. Fontaine. This was a government paper, issued at irregular intervals and at the discretion of the Spanish government. It was rather a vehicle of ordinances and public documents than a newspaper.

In the year 1803 an enterprising New-Englander named Lyons—a son of the celebrated Mathew Lyons—who had been sent to New-Orleans with despatches from government, on arriving there, and ascertaining that there was no regular press in the city, applied to General Wilkinson for patronage to establish a weekly paper. Herein he was successful; but, except himself, there was not another printer in New-Orleans, journeyman or "devil."

By some means, however, he learned that there were three young men[11] from the only printing office in Natchez, then belonging to the army, quartered in the city. He obtained their furlough from General Wilkinson—and obtaining the office of the "Moniteur," in a few weeks issued the first number of a paper entitled the "Union." To this in a few weeks succeeded the "Louisiana Courier," which, established in 1806, now holds a high rank in the army of periodicals, and is the oldest paper in the state.

The number of newspapers in the Territory of Orleans in 1810, was 10, (two of them daily;) all in the city of New-Orleans.

The number in Louisiana in 1828, was only nine. New-Orleans is the great centre of business and of publishing in this state. There are now published in New-Orleans seven daily papers, and 31 altogether in Louisiana.

SUMMARY

The Governor of Louisiana is elected by the people. Term begins January, 1835, and expires January 1839. Duration of the term, four years. Salary $7,500.

Senators, 17. Term of years, four. Representatives, 50. Term of years, two. Total—Senators and Representatives, 67. Pay per day, $4. Electors of president and vice president are chosen by general ticket.

Seat of government—New-Orleans. Time of holding elections—first Monday in July. Time of meeting of the legislature—first Monday in January.

Louisiana admitted into the Union in 1812.

Note B

"The State senators of Louisiana are elected for four years, one fourth vacating their seats annually. They must possess an estate of a thousand dollars in the parish, for which they are chosen. The representatives have a biennial term, and must possess 500 dollars' worth of property in the parish to be eligible. The governor is chosen for four years; and is ineligible for the succeeding term. His duties are the same, as in the other states, and his salary is 7,000 dollars a year. The judiciary powers are vested in a supreme and circuit court, together with a municipal court called the parish court.—The salaries are ample. The elective franchise belongs to every free white man of twenty-one years, and upward, who has had a residence of six months in the parish, and who has paid taxes.

The code of laws, adopted by this state, is not what is called the "common law," which is the rule of judicial proceedings in all the other states, but the *civil law*, adopted, with some modifications, from the judicial canons of France and Spain. So much of the common law is interwoven with it, as has been adopted by express deep stain upon the moral character to be generally reputed a cruel master. In many plantations no punishment is inflicted except after a trial by a jury, composed of the fellow-servants of the party accused. Festivals, prizes, and rewards are instituted, as stimulants to exertion, and compensations for superior accomplishment of labour. They are generally well fed and clothed, and that not by an arbitrary award, which might vary with the feelings of the master; but by periodical apportionment, like the distributed rations of soldiers, of what has been ascertained to be amply sufficient to render them comfortable.

Nor are they destitute, as has been supposed, of any legal protection, coming between them and the possible cupidity and cruelty of the masters. The '*code noir*' of Louisiana is a curious collection of statutes, drawn partly from French and Spanish law and usage, and partly from the customs of the islands, and usages, which have grown out of the peculiar circumstances of Louisiana while a colony. It has the aspect, it must be admitted, of being formed rather for the advantage of the master, than for the servant, for it prescribes an unlimited homage and obedience to the latter. But at the same time, it defines crimes, which the master can commit in relation to the slave, and prescribes the mode of trial, and the kind and degree of punishment. It constitutes unnecessary correction, maiming, and murder, punishable offences in a master. It is very minute in prescribing the number of hours, which the master may lawfully exact to be employed in labour, and the number of hours, which he must allow his slave for meal-time and for rest. It prescribes the time and extent of his holidays. In short, it settles with minuteness and detail the whole circle of relations between master and slave, defining, and prescribing what the former may, and may not exact from the latter.

That the slave is, also, in the general circumstances of his condition, as happy as this relation will admit of his being, is an unquestionable fact. That he seldom performs as much labour, or performs it as well as a free man, says all upon the subject of the motives which freedom only can supply, that can be alleged. In all the better managed plantations, the mode of building the quarters is fixed. The arrangement of the little village has a fashion by which it is settled. Interest, if not humanity, has defined the amount of food and rest, necessary for their health; and there is, in a large and respectable plantation, as much precision in the rules, as much exactness in the times of going to sleep, awaking, going to labour, and resting before and after meals, as in a garrison under military discipline, or in a ship of war. A bell gives all the signals; every slave, at the assigned hour in the morning, is forthcoming to his labour, or his case is reported, either as one of idleness, obstinacy, or sickness, in which case he is sent to the hospital, and there is attended by a physician, who, for the most part, has a yearly salary for attending to all the sick of the plantation. The union of physical force, directed by one will, is now well understood to have a much greater effect upon the amount of labour, which a number of hands, so managed, can bring about, than the same force directed by as many wills as there are hands. Hence it happens that while one free man, circumstances being the same, will perform more labour than one slave, a hundred slaves will accomplish more on one plantation, than so many hired free men, acting at their own discretion. Hence, too, it is, that such a prodigious quantity of cotton and sugar is made here, in proportion to the number of labouring hands. All the processes of agriculture are managed by system. Everything goes straight forward. There is no pulling down to-day the scheme of yesterday, and the whole amount of force is directed by the teaching of experience to the best result. *Flint's Miss. Val. Art. Louisiana*, vol. i. p. 527.

Note D.

"The borderers universally took an active part in the war, and were eminently useful in repelling the incursions of the Indians. Not even the most lawless but was found ready to pour out his life-blood for the republic.

A curious instance of the strange mixture of magnanimity and ferocity often found among the demi-savages of the borders was afforded by the Louisianian Lafitte. This desperado had placed himself at the head of a band of outlaws from all nations under heaven, and fixed his abode upon the top of an impregnable rock, to the south-west of the mouth of the Mississippi. Under the colours of the South American patriots, they pirated at pleasure every vessel that came in their way, and smuggled their booty up the secret creeks of the Mississippi, with a dexterity that baffled all the efforts of justice. The depredations of these outlaws, or, as they styled themselves, *Barritarians*, (from Barrita, their island,) becoming at length intolerable, the United States' government despatched an armed force against their little Tripoli. The establishment was broken up, and the pirates dispersed. But Lafitte again collected his outlaws, and took possession of his rock. The attention of the congress being now diverted by the war, he scoured the gulf at his pleasure, and so tormented the coasting traders, that Governor Claiborne of Louisiana set a price on his head.

This daring outlaw, thus confronted with the American government, appeared likely to promote the designs of its enemies. He was known to possess the clue to all the secret windings and entrances of the many-mouthed Mississippi; and in the projected attack upon New-Orleans it was deemed expedient to secure his assistance.

The British officer then heading the forces landed at Pensacola for the invasion of Louisiana, opened a treaty with the Barritarian, to whom he offered such rewards as were best calculated to tempt his cupidity and flatter his ambition. The outlaw affected to relish the proposal; but having artfully drawn from Colonel N—— the plan of his intended attack, he spurned his offers with the most contemptuous disdain, and instantly despatched one of his most trusty corsairs to the governor who had set a price for his life, advising him of the intentions of the enemy, and volunteering the aid of his little band, on the single condition that an amnesty should be granted for their past offences. Governor Claiborne, though touched by this proof of magnanimity, hesitated to close with the offer. The corsair kept himself in readiness for the expected summons, and continued to spy and report the motions of the enemy. As danger became more urgent, and the steady generosity of the outlaw more assured, Governor Claiborne granted to him and his followers life and pardon, and called them to the defence of the city. They obeyed with alacrity, and served with a valour, fidelity, and good conduct, not surpassed by the best volunteers of the republic."—*Flint's Miss. Valley.*

Note E.

The following extract from a narrative of the British attack on New-Orleans by Capt. Cooke, late of the British army, will, perhaps, not be without interest to many of my readers.

Camp before New-Orleans

"I do not remember ever looking for the first signs of day-break with more intense anxiety than on this eventful morning; every now and then I thought I heard the distant hum of voices, then again something like the doleful rustling of the wind before the coming storm, among the leaves of the foliage. But no; it was only the effect of the momentary buzzing in my ears; all was silent—the dew lay on the damp sod, and the soldiers were carefully putting aside their entrenching tools, and laying hold of their arms to be up and answer the first war-call at a moment's warning. How can I convey a thought of the intense anxiety of the mind, when a sombre silence is broken by the intonations of the cannon, and when the work of death begins? Now the veil of night was less obscured, and its murky mantle dissolved on all sides, and the mist sweeping off the face of the earth; yet it was not day, and no object was very visible beyond the extent of a few yards. The morn was chilly—I augured not of victory, an evil foreboding crossed my mind, and I meditated in solitary reflection. All was tranquil as the grave, and no camp-fires glimmered from either friends or foes.

Soon after this, two light companies of the seventh and ninety-third regiments came up without knapsacks, the highlanders with their blankets rolled and slung around their backs, and merely wearing the shell of their bonnets, the sable plumes of real ostrich feathers brought by them from the Cape of Good Hope, having been left in England. One company of the forty-third light infantry also followed, marching up rapidly. These three companies formed a compact little column of two hundred and forty soldiers, near the battery on the high road to New-Orleans. They were to attack the crescent battery near the river, and if possible to silence its fire under the muzzles of twenty pieces of cannon; at a point, too, where the bulk of the British force had hesitated when first they landed, and had recoiled from its fire on the twenty-eighth of last December, and on the first of January. I asked Lieut. Duncan Campbell where they were going, when he replied, "I'll be hanged if I know:" "then," said I, "you have got into what I call a good thing; a far-famed American battery is in front of you at a short range, and on the left of this spot is flanked, at 800 yards, by their batteries on the opposite bank of the river." At this piece of information he laughed heartily, and I told him to take off his blue pelisse-coat to be like the rest of the men. "No," he said gayly, "I will never peel for an American—come, Jack, embrace me." He was a fine young officer of twenty years of age, and had fought in many bloody encounters in Spain and France, but this was to be his last, as well as that of many more brave men. The mist was slowly clearing off, but objects could only be discerned at two or three hundred yards distance, as the morning was rather hazy; we had only quitted the battery two minutes, when a Congreve rocket was thrown up, whether from the enemy or not we could not tell; for some seconds it whizzed backward and forward in such a zigzag way, that we all looked up to see whether it was coming down upon our heads. The troops simultaneously halted, but all smiled at some sailors dragging a two-wheeled car a hundred yards to our left, which had brought up ammunition to the battery, who, by common consent, as it were, let go the shaft, and left it the instant the rocket was let off.—(This rocket, although we did not know it, proved to be the signal of attack.) All eyes were cast upward, like those of so many astronomers, to descry, if possible, what could be the upshot of this noisy harbinger, breaking in upon the solemn silence that reigned around. During all my military services I do not remember seeing a small body of troops thrown into such a strange configuration, having formed themselves into a circle, and halted, both officers and men, without any previous word of command, each man looking earnestly, as if by instinct of his imagination, to see in what particular quarter the anticipated firing would begin.

The Mississippi was not visible, its waters likewise being covered over with the fog; nor was there a single soldier, save our little phalanx, to be seen, or the tramp of a horse or a single footstep to be heard, by way of announcing that the battle-scene was about to begin, before the vapoury curtain was lifted or cleared away for the opposing forces to get a glimpse one of the other. So that we were completely lost, not knowing which way to bend our footsteps, and the only words which now escaped the officers were "steady, men," these precautionary warnings being quite unnecessary, as every soldier was, as it were, motionless like fox-hunters, waiting with breathless expectation, and casting significant looks one at the other before Reynard breaks cover.

All eyes seemed anxious to dive through the mist; and all ears attentive to the coming moment, as it was impossible to tell whether the blazing would begin from the troops who were supposed to have already crossed the river, or from the great battery of the Americans on the right bank of the Mississippi, or from the main lines. From all these points we were equidistant, and within point-blank range; and were left, besides, totally without orders, and without knowing how to act or where to find our own corps, just as if we had formed no part or parcel of the army.

The rocket had fallen probably in the Mississippi, all was silent, nor did a single officer or soldier attempt to shift his foot-hold, so anxiously were we all employed in listening for the first roar of the cannon to guide our footsteps, or as it were to pronounce with loud peals where was the point of our destination, well knowing that to go farther to the rear was not the way to find our regiment. This silence and suspense had not lasted more than two minutes, when the most vehement firing from the British artillery began opposite the left of the American lines, and before they could even see what objects they were firing at, or before the intended attacking column of the British were probably formed to go on to the assault. The American artillery soon responded, and thus it was that the gunners of the English and the Americans were firing through the mist at random; or in the supposed direction whence came their respective balls through the fog. And the first objects we saw, enclosed as it were in this little world of mist, were the cannon-balls tearing up the ground and crossing one another, and bounding along like so many cricket-balls through the air, coming on our left flank from the American batteries on the right bank of the river, and also from their lines in front.

At this momentous crisis a droll occurrence took place; a company of blacks emerged out of the mist, carrying ladders, which were intended for the three light companies for the left attack, but these Ethiopians were so confounded at the multiplicity of noises, that without farther ado, they dropped the ladders and fell flat on their faces, and without doubt, had their claws been of sufficient length, they would have scratched holes and buried themselves from such an unpleasant admixture of sounds and concatenation of iron projectiles, which seemed at war with one another, coming from two opposite directions at one and the same time.

If these blacks were only intended to carry the ladders to the three light companies on the left, they were too late. The great bulk of them were cut to pieces before the ladders were within reach of them; even if the best troops in the world had been carrying them, they would not have been up in time. This was very odd, and more than odd; it looked as if folly stalked abroad in the English camp. One or two officers went to the front in search of some responsible person to obtain orders *ad interim*; finding myself the senior officer, I at once, making a double as it were, or, as Napoleon recommended, marched to the spot where the heaviest firing was going on; at a run we neared the American line. The mist was now rapidly clearing away, but, owing to the dense smoke, we could not at first distinguish the attacking columns of the British troops to our right.

We now also caught a view of the seventh and the forty-third regiments in *echelon* on our right, near the wood, the royal fusileers being within about 300 yards of the enemy's lines, and the forty-third deploying into line 200 yards in *echelon* behind the fusileers. These two regiments were every now and then almost enveloped by the clouds of smoke that hung over their heads, and floated on their flanks, and the echo from the cannonade and musketry was so tremendous in the forests, that the vibration seemed as if the earth were cracking and tumbling to pieces, or as if the heavens were rent asunder by the most terrific peals of thunder that ever rumbled; it was the most awful and the grandest mixture of sounds to be conceived; the woods seemed to crack to an interminable distance, each cannon report was answered one hundred fold, and produced an intermingled roar surpassing strange. And this phenomenon can neither be fancied nor described, save by those who can bear evidence of the fact. And the flashes of fire looked as if coming out of the bowels of the earth, so little above its surface were the batteries of the Americans.

We had run the gauntlet, from the left to the centre in front of the American lines, under a cross fire, in hopes of joining in the assault, and had a fine view of the sparkling of the musketry, and the liquid flashes of the cannon. And melancholy to relate, all at once many soldiers were met wildly rushing out of the dense clouds of smoke, lighted up by a sparkling sheet of fire, which hovered over the ensanguined field. Regiments were shattered and dispersed—all order was at an end. And the dismal spectacle was seen of the dark shadows of men, like skirmishers, breaking out of the clouds of smoke, which majestically rolled along the even surface of the field. And so astonished was I at such a panic, that I said to a retiring soldier, "have we or the Americans attacked?" for I had never seen troops in such a hurry without being followed. "No," replied the man, with the countenance of despair, and out of breath, as he ran along, "we attacked, sir." For still the reverberation was so intense toward the great wood, that any one would have thought the great fighting was going on there instead of immediately in front.

Lieut. Duncan Campbell, of our regiment, was seen to our left running about in circles, first staggering one way, then another, and at length fell upon the sod helplessly on his face, and again tumbled, and when he was picked up, he was found to be blind from the effect of grape-shot, which had torn open his forehead, giving him a slight wound in the leg, and also ripped the scabbard from his side, and knocked the cap from his head. While being borne insensible to the rear, he still clenched the hilt of his sword with a convulsive grasp, the blade thereof being broken off close at the hilt with grape-shot, and in a state of delirium and suffering he lived for a few days.

The first officer we met was Lieutenant-Colonel Stovin, of the staff, who was unhorsed, without his hat, and bleeding down the left side of his face. He at first thought the two hundred were the whole regiment, and he said, "Forty-third, for God's sake save the day!" Lieutenant-Colonel Smith of the rifles, and one of Packenham's staff, then rode up at full gallop from the right, (he had a few months before brought to England the despatches of the capture of Washington) and said to me, "Did you ever see such a scene?—There is nothing left but the seventh and forty third! just draw up here for a few minutes, to show front, that the repulsed troops may re-form." For the chances now were, as the greater portion of the actually attacking corps were stricken down, and the remainder dispersed, that the Americans would become the assailants. The ill-fated rocket was discharged before the British troops moved on; the consequence was, that every American gun was warned by such a silly signal to be laid on the parapets, ready to be discharged with the fullest effect.

The misty field of battle was now inundated with wounded officers and soldiers, who were going to the rear from the right, left, and centre; in fact, little more than one thousand soldiers were left unscathed out of the three thousand who attacked the American lines, and they fell like the very blades of grass beneath the scythe of the mower. Packenham was killed; Gibbes was mortally wounded; his brigade dispersed like the dust before the whirlwind, and Keane was wounded. The command of his Majesty's forces at this critical juncture now fell to Major-general Lambert, the only general left, and he was in reserve with his fine brigade.

The rifle corps individually took post to resist any forward movements of the enemy, but the ground already named being under a cross fire of at least twenty pieces of artillery, the advantage was all on the side of the Americans, who in a crowd might have completely run down a few scattered troops, exposed to such an overpowering force of artillery. The black troops behaved in the most shameful manner to a man, and, although hardly exposed to fire, were in abominable consternation, lying down in all directions. One broad beaver, with the ample folds of the coarse blanket, thrown across the shoulders of the Americans, was as terrible in their eyes as a panther might be while springing among a timid multitude. These black corps, it is said, had behaved well at some West India islands, where the thermometer was more congenial to their feelings. Lieut. Hill (now Capt. Hill) said, in his shrewd manner, "Look at the seventh and the forty-third, like seventy-fours becalmed!" As soon as the action was over, and some troops were formed in our rear, we then, under a smart fire of grape and round shot, moved to the right, and joined our own corps, which had been ordered to lie down at the edge of the ditch; and some of the old soldiers, with rage depicted on their countenances, were demanding why they were not led on to the assault. The fire of the Americans, from behind their barricades, had been indeed so murderous, and had caused so sudden a repulse, that it was difficult to persuade ourselves that such an event had happened—the whole affair being more like a dream, or some scene of enchantment, than reality.

And thus it was: on the left bank of the river, three generals, seven colonels, and seventy five officers, making a total of seventeen hundred and eighty-one officers and soldiers, had fallen in a few minutes.

The royal fusileers and the Monmouthshire light infantry, from the beginning to the end of the battle, were astounded at the ill success of the combat; and while formed within grape range, were lost in amazement at not being led on to the attack, being kept as quiet spectators of the onslaught.

About an hour and a half after the principal attack had failed, we heard a rapid discharge of fire-arms, and a few hurried sounds of cannon on the right bank of the river, when all was again silent, until three distinct rounds of British cheers gladdened our ears from that direction, although at least one mile and a quarter from where we were stationed. They were Colonel Thornton's gallant troops, who were successful in the assault on the American works in that quarter, the details of which, for a brief space, I must postpone.

For *five* hours the enemy plied us with grape and round shot; some of the wounded lying in the mud or on wet grass, managed to crawl away; but every now and then some unfortunate man was lifted off the ground by round shot, and lay killed or mangled.—During the tedious hours we remained in front, it was necessary to lie on the ground, to cover ourselves from the projectiles. An officer of our regiment was in a reclining posture, when a grape-shot passed through both his knees; at first he sank back faintly, but at length opening his eyes, and looking at his wounds, he said, "Carry me away. I am *chilled to death;*" and as he was hoisted on the men's shoulders, more round and grape shot passed his head; taking off his hat, he waved it; and after many narrow escapes, got out of range, suffered amputation of both legs, and died of his wounds on ship-board, after enduring all the pain of the surgical operation, and passing down the lake in an open boat.

A wounded soldier, who was lying among the slain, two hundred yards behind us, continued, without any cessation, for two hours, to raise his arm up and down with a convulsive motion, which excited the most painful sensations among us; and as the enemy's balls now and then killed or maimed some soldiers, we could not help casting our eyes toward the moving arm, which really was a dreadful magnet of attraction; it even caught the attention of the enemy, who, without seeing the body, fired several round shot at it. A black soldier lay near us, who had received a blow from a cannon-ball, which had obliterated all his features; and although blind, and suffering the most terrible anguish, he was employing himself in scratching a hole to put his money into. A tree, about two feet in diameter and fifteen in height, with a few scattered branches at the top, was the only object to break the monotonous scene. This tree was near the right of our regiment; the Americans, seeing some persons clustering around it, fired a thirty-two pound shot, which struck the tree exactly in the centre, and buried itself in the trunk with a loud concussion. Curiosity prompted some of us to take a hasty inspection of it, and I could clearly see the rusty ball within the tree. I thrust my arm in a little above the elbow joint, and laid hold of it; it was truly amazing, between the intervals of firing the cannon, to see the risks continually run by the officers to take a peep at this good shot. Owing to this circumstance, the vicinity of the tree became rather a hot berth; but the American gunners failed to hit it a second time, although some balls passed very near on each side, and for an hour it was a source of excessive jocularity to us. In the middle of the day a flag of truce was sent by Gen. Lambert to Gen. Jackson, to be allowed to bury the dead, which was acceded to by the latter on certain conditions."

Note F.

To the politeness of Dr. William Dunbar, a planter of Mississippi, the author is indebted for many important papers relating to this region, formerly in the possession of his father—a gentleman well known to the philosophic world as the author of several valuable scientific papers upon the natural history and meteorology of this country. Among the manuscripts of this gentleman in the author's possession, is the following account of the manufacture of Indigo, written by himself, then an extensive indigo planter, near New-Orleans.

"The reservoir water in or near the field where the indigo plant is cultivated, is prepared, in lower Louisiana, by digging a canal from eighty to one hundred feet long, and 25 or 30 feet wide. The plant is in its strength when in full blossom: it is then cut down, and disposed regularly in a wooden or brick vault, about ten feet square, and three feet deep; water is then poured or pumped over it until the plant is covered; it is suffered to remain until it has undergone a fermentation, analogous to the vinous fermentation. If it stands too long, a second fermentation commences, bearing affinity to the acetous fermentation: your liquor is then spoiled, and will yield you but little matter of a bad quality—sometimes none at all. The great difficulty is to know this proper point of fermentation, which cannot sometimes be ascertained to any degree of certainty; when the plant is rich, and the weather warm, a tolerable judgment may be formed by the ascent or swelling of the liquor in the vat; at other times no alteration is observed. But to return; the liquor is at length drawn off into another vat, called the beater; it may remain in the first vat, called the steeper, from ten to fifteen hours, and even twenty-four hours, in the cool weather of autumn. The liquor is agitated in the beater in a manner similar to the churning of butter; when first drawn off, it is of a pale straw colour, but gradually turns to a pale green, from thence to a deeper green, and at length to a deep blue. This is occasioned by the grains of indigo, at first dissolved in the water, and afterward extricated by beating. The indigo is now ready to fall to the bottom by its superior specific gravity; but a precipitant is often used to cause a more hasty decomposition, and consequent precipitation. This is effected most powerfully by lime-water, but it may also be done by any mucilaginous substance, as the juice of the wild mallows, purslain, leaves of the elm-tree, and of many others indigenous in this country. The saliva produces the same effects. A few hours after the precipitation, the water standing above the indigo is drawn off by holes perforated for that purpose; the indigo matter is then swept out and farther drained, either by putting it in bags of Russia duck, or more commodiously in wooden cases with a bottom of cloth; after which it is put in a wooden frame, with a loose Osnaburg cloth between it and the frame, and subjected to a considerable press—light at first, but heavy at the last; and when solid enough, cut into squares, which shrink up in drying to half their first bulk. After it appears to be dry, it is put up in heaps to sweat and dry the second time; it is then fit for market. All that has not been injured by missing the true point of fermentation, sells here generally at a dollar a pound. The planter often, by mistake, makes his indigo of a superior quality, so as to be equal to the Guatemala indigo, and be worth from one dollar and a quarter to two dollars. This happens from the indigo maker's drawing off his water from the steeper too soon, before it has arrived at its due point of fermentation. In this case the quantity is so much lessened, as by no means to render the planter compensated by the superior quality. The grand desideratum to bring the making of indigo to some degree of certainty, is the discovery of some chymical test, that shall demonstrate the passing of the liquor from the first to the second fermentation. This test will probably be discovered in some saline body, but which, or in what quantity, it is yet difficult to ascertain."

Note G.

The following additional observations upon New-Orleans, its parish, and neighbourhood, convey, at a glance, the general resources of this region of country, besides containing much information not embodied in the work:—

"The parish of Orleans includes the city. Chef Menteur, Rigolets, Bayou Bienvenu, Bayou Gentilly, and Bayou St. Johns, are all in this parish, and are famous in the history of the late war, Lake Pontchartrain, lake Borgne, Barataria bay, gulf of Mexico, Caminda bay, lake Des Islets, lake Rond, Little lake, and Quacha lake, are in the limits of this parish. Sugar, and after that, cotton, are the staples. Along the coast there are groves of orange-trees, and the fig is extensively raised. In this parish are the greater part of the defences, that are intended to fortify the city of New-Orleans against the attack of a foreign foe. The chief fortifications are on those points, by which the British approached toward the city during the late war. Extensive fortifications of brick have been erected at Petits Coquilles, Chef Menteur, and Bayou Bienvenu, the two former guarding the passes of the Rigolet, between lake Borgne and lake Pontchartrain, and the latter the approach from lake Borgne toward New-Orleans. A great work, to mount 120 cannon, is erecting at Placquemine on the Mississippi. These works, when finished, will not fall far short of the expense 2,000,000 dollars. Fort St. Johns, at the entrance of the Bayou St. Johns into lake Pontchartrain, is well situated for the defence of the pass. It is an ancient establishment of the former regime. The guns are of vast calibre; but they appear to be sealed, and the walls have a ruinous aspect. These points of defence have been selected with great judgment, and have been fortified with so much care, that it is supposed no enemy could ever again approach the city by the same passes, through which it was approached by the British in the past war. New-Orleans, the key of the Mississippi valley, and the great depot of its agriculture and commerce, is already a city of immense importance, and is every year becoming more so. This city has strong natural defences, in its position and its climate. It is now strongly defended by artificial fortifications. But, after all, the best defence of this, and of all other cities, is the vigilant and patriotic energy of the battalions of free men, who can now, by steamboats, be brought down to its defence in a few days from the remotest points of the west. It is not to be forgotten, that by the same conveyance, an enemy might also be brought against it.

Of the other parishes, we may remark, in general, that as far up the Mississippi as the parish of Baton Rouge, on the east side, and Point Coupee on the west, the cultivation of the sugar-cane is the chief pursuit of the inhabitants. The same may be said of Placquemine, Lafourche, and Attakapas. The staple article of the western parishes beyond is cotton.

The parishes north of lake Pontchartrain, which formerly made a part of Florida, with the exception of some few tracts, and the alluvions of Pearl river and Bogue Chitte, have a sterile soil. The inhabitants raise large herds of cattle, and send great quantities of lumber to New-Orleans, together with pitch, tar, turpentine and coal. They burn great quantities of lime from the beds of shells, which cover large tracts near the lakes; they also send sand from the beaches of the lakes, for covering the pavements of New-Orleans. They have also, for some years past, manufactured brick to a great amount, and have transported them across the lake. They have a great number of schooners that ply on the lakes, in this and other employments. The people engaged in this extensive business, find the heavy tolls demanded on the canal a great impediment in the way of the profit of this trade.[12] The country generally is covered with open pine woods, and has small tracts of second-rate land interspersed among these tracts. The country is valuable from its inexhaustible supplies of timber and wood for the New-Orleans market.

FOOTNOTES

[11] These were George Cooper—Elijah W. Brown, now a wealthy planter in Monroe, Washita, La. and I. K. Cook, for many years post a leading editor in this state.

[12] The rail-road is now the medium of conveyance for these articles of produce to the city; the expense is thereby much lessened, and the facilities for this trade increased.